THE SELF CONFIDENCE AND SELF ESTEEM WORKBOOK

Cognitive Behavioral Therapy Guide for Men and Women to Overcoming Self-Doubt and Improve Self-Critic

DR. HARRY VITALE

Disclaimer Notice

Please note the information contained within this document is for educational and entertainment purposes only. All effort has been executed to present accurate, up to date, and reliable, complete information. No warranties of any kind are declared or implied. Readers acknowledge that the author is not engaging in the rendering of legal, financial, medical or professional advice. The content within this book has been derived from various sources. Please consult a licensed professional before attempting any techniques outlined in this book.

By reading this document, the reader agrees that under no circumstances is the author responsible for any losses, direct or indirect, which are incurred as a result of the use of information contained within this document, including, but not limited to, — errors, omissions, or inaccuracies.

Contents

Introduction

In the pages ahead, you will learn how to build confidence, bravery and unshakeable resolve in every area of your life. You will learn to face the most significant challenges and opportunities of your life without fear, confident of your abilities to do whatever you believe you can.

The good news is that you have an incredible potential for success, accomplishment, and wealth, with more creativity and natural ability than you could have in a hundred lifetimes. The only thing that lies between you and the wonderful future that is imaginable for you is fear of all sorts, and by the time you finish this book, your fears will be gone forever.

I've been researching influential men and women for many years, searching for the traits and attributes they have in common that have allowed them to do so much more than the average person. I've read thousands of books, essays, and studies on success, and I've come to the conclusion that the cornerstone of success in every walk of life is self-confidence. Each man or woman who has ever done anything outside the normal has turned out to have greater self-confidence than the ordinary person. Confidence is a term that we often use in everyday language, but never can we stop thinking of what it means. Confidence consists of optimistic hopes of positive outcomes. Confidence influences the willingness to invest-to devote cash, time, credibility, emotional energy, or other resources-or to withhold or hedge investment. This spending, or its lack, forms the ability to make a difference. In that sense, trust lies at the heart of civilization. Everything about an economy, a society, an organization or a team depends on it. Every action we take, every commitment we make, is dependent on whether we think we can count on ourselves and others to do what has been planned. Confidence dictates whether our actions, personally or in a group, are small and hesitant or broad and confident.

Often our minds can get the best of us, making it hard to be self-confident or self-reliant. We all have an unconscious criticism that overloads our brains with past and future flaws and feelings. The inner critic is that silent voice which overloads us with negative thoughts, stress, and opinions which underestimates us and tells us we can't do anything. Hearing this inner voice could hamper our ability to manage and deal with stress or other problems that life throws our way. When we continue to believe our inner critic for a long time, our self-esteem and self-image will be skewed, which can cause high amounts of pressure, leading to depression and anxiety.

Most of the people feel bad about themselves from time to time. Feelings of low self-esteem may be caused by someone else's poor treatment recently or in the past, or by a person's own opinion of himself or herself. It's natural. Nevertheless, low self-esteem is a constant companion for too many people, particularly those who experience depression, anxiety, phobias, paranoia, delirious thought, illness or disability. If you are one of these men, you may have to go through life feeling bad about yourself. Low self-esteem prevents you from enjoying life, doing the things you want to do, and working towards personal goals.

You've got the right to feel good for yourself. Nonetheless, it can be very difficult to feel better for yourself when you are under stress of having problems that are difficult to manage, when you are coping with a disease, when you are having a difficult time, and when others are treating you poorly. At this time, it is easy to be pulled into a downward spiral of lower and lower self-esteem. Of starters, you could start feeling worse about yourself when someone hurts you, you're under a lot of pressure at work, or you're having a hard time getting along with someone in your family. So you begin to give yourself negative self-talk, like "I'm not healthy." This may make you feel so bad about yourself that you do something to harm yourself or someone else, such as getting drunk or shouting at your kids. By using the tips and exercises in this manual, you will stop doing things that make you feel even worse and do things that make you feel good about yourself.

Its guide will bring you ideas about things you can do to make you feel better about yourself-to increase your self-esteem. The ideas came from people like yourself, individuals who know they have a low self-esteem and are working to improve it. When you continue to use the techniques in this manual and other strategies you might think of to boost your self-esteem, you might find that you have some feelings of aversion to positive feelings for yourself. It's natural. Don't let those emotions stop you from feeling good for yourself. They're going to decrease because you feel better and better for yourself. To help relieve those emotions, Let your buddies know what you're going through. If you can, have a good cry. Do things you need to relax, such as meditating and taking a nice warm bath.

While you read this manual and focus on the exercises, keep in mind the following statement:

"I am a very different, exceptional and important person. I deserve to feel better about myself."

Self Confidence Identification

THERE ARE different chapters in Part One of this self-confidence workbook that describe what self-confidence is and all facets of self-esteem. On a deeper level, you can know yourself and benefit from where self-confidence and self-esteem come from. You will learn that your self-esteem and confidence will grow by offering yourself kindness, empathy, and affection. Have you ever wondered why you feel like you're on the right track, then something knocks you down and you're three steps back from where you've been? This can occur due to low levels of self-esteem and trust. Yes, it's special. When you learn how to incorporate self-respect in your life, you will begin to see the obstacles in your life that will stop you from climbing the ladder of success. You may step out of the darkness and become the light of your own life with the power of positivity and using several ways to overcome your inner critical voice.

These next three chapters will give you a clearer description about self-confidence, self-love, self-respect, self-worth, self-esteem, and care. Each is different in its own sense and ties together to decide what self-esteem and self-confidence should be. One thing is certain the ongoing critical voice that connects you within your head can never be sure. The first step is, therefore, to resolve the "negative Nancy" and seek a deeper meaning in order to motivate you to live the life you deserve.

Comprehending Yourself

KNOWING who you are is the most critical step in building self-confidence and self-esteem. Believe it or not, many people do not even know who they are and are struggling to figure it out. This section encourages you to discover yourself and figure out who you are on a deeper level so you can appreciate what works best for you when you actually commit to personal growth and find ways to get what you want. Did you ask why you've been angry without any reason? You may not enjoy your job, but you may wonder why you are there. Have you ever argued over things that seem needless with your spouse? Much of our unconscious responses derive from our subconscious mind, which influences our behavior to a large extent. When you better understand yourself (what makes you do what you do and what you think, the way you do it), you will gain a better understanding of how to make better decisions, leading to greater self-confidence.

There are a couple of steps to learning how to understand yourself better:

Get an overview of yourself

YOU CAN ASK some of your friends and family members about a feedback about who they believe you are, but this can lead to prejudices you already have. You can do a few personality tests, such as the Myer-Briggs personality test, instead of searching about, or you can study the nine basic types of personality through the enneagram test.

The definition of personality analysis by Myers-Briggs describes seventeen different types of personality into which you might come. The assessments consist of eight different types of people that you can be intro-vert/extrovert, sensing/intuition, thinking/feeling, and judging/perceiving, based on your responses. The findings will clarify which of the 16 characteristics in which you belong. For example, you would fall into ENFJ to be an extrovert, emotional, thinking, and judgmental person.

The enneagram scale is a bit more complicated and requires a bit of understanding; nevertheless, it is made up of nine different types of personalities in which you fall. This consists of a graph that describes personal growth and where and how to get to where you want to be on the scale. The enneagram doesn't suit you into a particular category because it leaves room for you to develop into any type of personality. As frustrating as these assessments may be, you may be able to understand yourself a little more thoroughly by studying or taking a personality test.

Perform reading assignments on individuality/personality

A PERSONALITY WRITING exercise is what novel writers are going to do in order to have a better picture of the personalities they want to explore in their novels. You will find some examples online, and this project's aim is to learn about things you didn't know about yourself. Some of the outlines of character consist of asking if a person has any behaviors or "ticks" that may distinguish them from the world, such as nail-biting, or if they have an accent. Below are some questions you can ask yourself:

- How do you describe yourself?
- What's your goal?
- What's the most important thing you've ever done?
- What's the most embarrassing thing you've ever experienced?
- What do you worry most about?
- Who are you most appreciating and valuing?
- Who separates you from others?
- What is a life-changing moment for you?

YOU WILL GAIN A BETTER understanding of who you are by addressing these specific questions.

Define your abilities and weaknesses

THROUGH ANALYZING and thinking specifically about your strengths and weaknesses, you can find out what is most important in your writing exercise to help you answer the questions you have struggled with. Compare your experience with your strengths and weaknesses with your friends and family's strengths and weaknesses. This can help you to understand more about yourself and how you see and feel about yourself.

Many strength examples are committed, dedicated, strong, decisive, and coordinated. There are some examples of weaknesses that are narrow-minded, greedy, insecure and judgmental.

Assess your goals and what matters to you

YOUR PRIORITIES STEM down to your beliefs, morals, and values. When you think about these things, you can determine what is most important to you. Here are a few things to consider when determining your priorities:

- If your house is on fire, what is the first thing that comes to your mind that you will save? These can be anything from tax papers to memorabilia.
- If someone is living a lifestyle that you don't agree with, like veganism or transsexualism (just an example), how would you respond? Even though you don't agree, would you still be supportive? Would you protect them? How?
- What is most important to you? Some examples of things that people mostly prioritize are money, family, respect, and stability.

In understanding yourself on a deeper level, you will be able to experience more happiness and self-control. You will be able to make wiser decisions. You will have resilience during stressful events, and you will gain a deeper understanding of others. Many benefits come with understanding yourself. Now let us learn what self-confidence and self-esteem are.

Look how you've improved

LOOK at your history and talk about how what's happened to you throughout your life has influenced what you act and think now. Talking at how you've evolved as a person will say a lot about why you're acting the way you're doing, as our new habits are based on our past experiences.

Of starters, you may start to get really angry against shoplifters, and you're very hard on people you see as cheating. If you thought about it, you might remember stealing a cookie from a supermarket as a kid, and your parents are punishing you very severely, which would explain your more than a normal reaction to that crime now.

Below are things you can find out about yourself by taking the "learning type" personality test?

- The kind of intra-personal problems or weaknesses you have.
- What your goals are.
- Why you excel in some issues and compete with others.

- What kind of sports or interests you find satisfying.

ANALIZING YOUR MIND
AND ACTIONS

Check yourself if you have strong emotions

SOMETIMES YOU'LL FIND yourself getting really, really mad, sad, happy, and excited. Knowing what causes these Stronger-than-normal reactions, what their root cause is, will help you better understand yourself.

For example, you might get really angry about people talking in a film. Are you really mad at talking or are you upset that you thought it was a direct sign of disrespect to you? Since this rage doesn't help the situation, you might be better off trying to find ways that you can be less concerned about people who trust you, just to keep your blood pressure down.

Look out for persecution and transfer

REPRESSION IS when you don't want to talk about something, so you can let yourself forget what happened. Transference is when you react emotionally to one thing, but what you really react to is something else. Both of these very normal habits is unhealthful and figuring out why you do them, and learning ways to handle those feelings more healthily, will make you a much happier person.

You might feel, for example, that you're not sorry about your grandma dying, but when your family decides to get rid of her favorite old chair, you get really angry and upset. You're not really mad that the seat is gone. It was dirty, smelled bad, and probably what you knew is toxic foam. You're sad that your grandma's dead.

Remember how and when you're thinking about yourself

SHOULD you turn every conversation you've had into a discussion with yourself? Do you make jokes at your own expense when you think about yourself? How and when you talk about yourself will reveal a lot about how you think about yourself and how you feel about yourself. It's nice to worry to yourself sometimes, and it's great to realize that you can't do it all, but you should pay attention to extremes and care about why you're going to extremes like that.

Your friend might have just completed her Ph.D., for example, but when you're both thinking about it, you turn the topic to when you're focused on your master's. This might be because you feel embarrassed that you've only earned a master's degree and that you've done a Ph.D., so you want to make yourself feel more important and competent by thinking about you.

Look at how and why you're communicating with others

WILL you tend to put them down when you interact with people? You may have found that you only choose to spend time with people who have more money than you do. Behaviors like this can tell you things about yourself and what's really important to you.

For example, if you choose to spend time with friends who have more money than you do, it might indicate that you want to feel better by encouraging yourself to believe that you are superior to your friends in that way.

Talk about what you "hear" from what you said. This is another thing you should look for when you evaluate your relationships with friends and family. You might think that what you say is something like "I want your support" when what they actually said was "I need your company," showing that you have a tremendous need to sound helpful to others.

Write down your biography

WRITE a biography of 500 words in 20 minutes. This will allow you to type very easily and care less about what you're going to include, allowing you to define what your brain thinks is most important when it comes to identifying who you are. For a lot of people, 20 minutes won't be enough time to write 500 letters. Thinking about what you're angry, you haven't been able to get away with what you said can also tell you things about yourself.

Meditation

TAKE 10-15 minutes in the morning or at night to relax your mind and concentrate on the emotions that go through your brain. Practice deep breathing, sit in a calm environment, and note the ideas that come to you spontaneously.

When you find harmony within yourself, you will be more linked to your inner being, which is a good part of understanding yourself better.

See how long you will wait to be paid

STUDIES HAVE SHOWN that people who can postpone gratification, usually, have a better time to get through their careers, get better grades, get more jobs, and keep a healthier body. Talk of circumstances where you might have lost gratification. What have you done? If you're having trouble resisting pleasure, this is something to watch out for, because it often plays a role in performance.

Stanford had a famous experiment called the Marshmallow, where they watched several children respond when they were treated with marshmallow therapies and then tracked their life-long success over many decades. Children who gave up care in favor of higher incentives did better in school, jobs, and health-related areas.

Take a look at whether you need to ask or be told

WHEN YOU DO SOMETHING, like school, think about whether you're looking for your next job without having to worry, do you need someone else to tell you what to do before you do it, or whether you'd just miss it all in favor of just asking someone else what to do. Each of these things will teach you different things about you, depending on the situation.

Note, there's nothing wrong with someone giving you directions and feedback before you do a job. It's just something you need to be mindful of so that you can better understand and control your own actions if important things happen. For example, when you know you're bad at taking control of a situation, however, you know you need to, you should talk about how your resistance is just a "habit" that you can shake, not a need.

Look at the way you're responding in tough and fresh conditions

IF TIMES GET REALLY DIFFICULT, like when you lose your job, a loved one dies, or someone attacks you, the more secret and reserved aspects of your personality tend to come forward. Talk about how you responded in the past when the pressure was heavy. How did you react the way you did it? How would you like you to react? Would you be more likely to react like that now?

You can also envision these possibilities, but be mindful that your theoretical responses may be clouded by your prejudice and may not be reliable as to how you would respond.

Imagine, for instance, that you were moving to a new area where no one knows you. Where are you going to make friends? What kind of people would you be trying to make friends with? Is there anything you'd alter from what you tell people about yourself to what all your new friends know about you? This could show your interests and what you're looking for in your social interactions.

Think about how force affects your actions

IF YOU ARE in any kind of power position, you might want to think about the effect it has on your actions. Most men, if placed in a position of power, will become stronger, less open-minded, more commanding, and more suspicious. If you find yourself making decisions that affect others, think about why you really made the choice: is it because it's the right thing to do, or is it because you need to feel uncontrollable about the situation?

For example, when you're babysitting your little boy, are you putting him in time for a small problem? Does this really help him learn, or are you just trying to find a way to get him out of time?

Take a look at the causes

THINGS THAT AFFECT what you feel and how you see the world can say a lot about you, whether you actually follow what they mean or not. You can better understand the origin of the patterns you have when you see how the experiences have influenced your actions. You can also recognize your personality and your own individual beliefs by seeing how you deviate from those patterns taught.

Thinks of the influence that you include:

- Your entertainment content, such as TV shows, films, books, and even what porn you watch.
- Your parents, who may teach you things that vary from tolerance to racism to material wealth to spiritual wealth.
- Your family, who are going to push you to do other things and expose you to new and wonderful experiences.

OPENING UP FOR REFLECTION

13

Just let go of that defensiveness

IF YOU REALLY WANT TO ANALYZE AND know yourself better, you're going to have to think about aspects of yourself that you really don't want, or confess to some stuff that you might not want to accept. You'll obviously be stubborn about admitting those kinds of things to yourself, but if you're ever going to understand how you work, then you're going to have to let go of that defensiveness. Even if you don't let the walls down for other men, at least you have to let them down for yourself.

Being less guarded about your shortcomings can also mean opening yourself to other people's help and making amends for past mistakes. If you are more open to discussion, criticism, and change, then other people can really help you understand and improve yourself.

14

Be frank to yourself

WE LIE to ourselves a bit more than we would like to talk about sometimes. We're going to help ourselves feel that we made some questionable choices for moral and logical reasons, even when we were just vindictive and lazy. Yet hiding behind our reasons from the real reason doesn't encourage us to improve and grow into better people. Remember: there's no point lying to yourself. Even if you learn the facts about yourself that you really don't like, it just gives you the chance to face those issues head-on instead of just pretend they don't exist.

React to what others are asking you about yourself

SOMETIMES, especially when we do bad things, others will try to warn us against this kind of behavior. They also tend not to listen. Sometimes this is great, because a lot of people are going to say things to you just because they want to harm you, because their words are going to have no basis in fact. But sometimes what they claim is a nice, outsider study of how you act. Talk about what people have said in the past and ask for new feedback about your actions.

Your sister might note, for instance, that you tend to exaggerate. But this is unintentional on your part, which can serve to show you that your perception of reality is a bit off the mark.

There is a big difference between hearing what people think about you and having that belief to control your life and behavior. You're not expected to change your actions to suit other people unless it has a significant negative impact on your life (and even then, you might want to acknowledge that your atmosphere might be a concern, not your behavior). Make changes because you want to change things, not because someone else wants you to change things.

Give some advice

GIVING advice will often give you a great opportunity to think through your own challenges and re-evaluate them from outside. Talking at someone else's case, you're more likely to think of situations and circumstances you've never thought about before.

You don't even have to do this event for real, because supporting your peers, relatives, and even strangers is a good thing to do. In the form of a letter, you can give advice to your older and younger self. This will allow you to look through your past experiences and what you've taken away from them, as well as what's most important to you for the future.

16

Take your time to live your life

THE BEST WAY to really get to know yourself, though, is to experience life. Just like getting to know someone else, knowing yourself takes time, and you're going to learn a lot more by experiencing life than by questioning yourself or taking tests. You could try:

Traveling: Traveling will put you in a lot of different situations and test your ability to cope with stress and adapt to change. You're going to get a better understanding of your happiness, priorities, and dreams than you've ever been able to sit in the same old, boring life.

Getting further education right now: Training, real education, pushes us to learn in a new way. Having training will open your mind and allow you to think about things you'd never thought of before. Your passions and how you feel about the new things you're discovering will reveal things about you.

Letting go of your hopes: Let go of the aspirations of other people for you. Let go of your expectations of yourself. Let go of your expectations as to what life should be like. When you do this, you will be more open to seeing what new experiences could make you happy and satisfied. Life is a wild roller coaster, and you're going to face a lot of things which scare you because they're new or different, but you're not going to be close to those encounters. They could make you happier than you have ever been.

Understanding Self Confidence

SELF-CONFIDENCE IS an approach to your strengths and weaknesses. This means that you accept and respect yourself and have a sense of control in your life. You know your strengths and weaknesses well, and you have a positive view of yourself. You set realistic goals and priorities, negotiate assertively, and can handle criticism.

On the other hand, low self-confidence can make you feel full of self-doubt, passive and submissive, or have difficulty trusting others. You may feel inferior, unloved, and critical. Feeling confident can depend on the situation. For example, you can feel very confident in some fields, such as education, but lack confidence in others, such as relationships.

On the other hand, low self-confidence can make you feel full of self-doubt, passive and submissive, or have difficulty trusting others. You may feel inferior, unloved, and critical. Feeling confident can depend on the situation. For example, you can feel very confident in some fields, such as education, but lack confidence in others, such as relationships.

Through default, "trust" is a state in which somebody believes some reality about something. Trust is when someone can dive into something with the absolute belief that all will be well and good. This is one's self-assurance that things are going to happen properly. It's 100% self-confident in the values. This can happen absolutely when someone respects himself and realizes who he is as a person. It's when you feel good about yourself and fully trust your skills. Self-confidence comes from three qualities that everyone has, which are as follows: the ability to think positively about yourself and your environment, the ability to be fully certain that you bring positive value into your life and have trust in all your skills (regardless of what others feel and think about you) the ability to continue to think positively about yourself and your situation. These are all forms of positive thinking. So to be a self-confident person, you need to get complete positivity while understanding when to acknowledge the negative as well.

Most people, like the future, are trying to control what is impossible to control. When we're busy trying to control the future, instead of realizing it hasn't happened yet, we're left dwelling on the bad. Feeling optimistic is understanding when you can control things and when you can deal on things you can't.

The thing to remember with self-confidence is that it's neither right nor wrong, but it's very helpful to have it. Just as a full or empty glass is neither right nor wrong, it is neither right nor wrong when you lack self-confidence. One of the most beneficial things to be positive in is that you get stronger and wiser than poorer and feel stuck in the same position through every encounter. By this, I mean, you're expected to feel rejected and humiliated when you have low self-confidence, which makes it harder to handle situations. That being said, you may not be able to "put yourself out there for fear of being judged or dismissed." In this way, you grow weaker and weaker over time because you are becoming more and more afraid to do the things you need. You wouldn't take risks required to lead a fulfilling and satisfying life because of low self-confidence.

Here are the advantages of having a high degree of self-confidence: greater regard for yourself and your self-worth, more satisfaction and gratitude, less self-doubt, less depression and less fear of failure, more motivation and commitment to work for better overall physical and mental health. The little stuff doesn't matter to you when you have self-confidence. You are not afraid of being ignored or punished, as you know yourself. You have high self-respect, and you're not breaking that move by someone else's judgment. The second part of this book explains and shows you how to do this if you want to learn how to build your self-esteem and be more self-confident as an adult.

While self-confidence can mean different things to different people, in fact, it simply means having faith in oneself.

Confidence is, in part, the product of how we were brought up and educated. We hear from others how to feel about ourselves and how to act-these experiences have an effect on what we believe about ourselves and others. Confidence is also the product of our experience and how we have learned to adapt to different situations.

Self-confidence is not a percentage indicator. The trust in fulfilling roles and activities and coping with problems will increase and decrease, and some days we may feel more confident than others.

I would like to share with you five reasons why you need to build your self-confidence.

Self-confidence makes you attractive

WOULD YOU LIKE TO LIVE THE LIFE OF YOUR DREAMS?

Do you want to be a man with wealth?

- You need to be able to bring the right kind of people into your world.
- You've got to learn how to be self-assured.
- People are attracted to self-assured customers.

WHEN YOU WALKED INTO A ROOM, which one of these two people would you be drawn to? The man standing in the corner with a smile on his face, or the lady whose head is bowed, looking down at her mobile.

You'd be drawn to the man!

You're more appealing when you're self-confident!

Self-confidence has you recruited for your dream careers or customers

IF YOU WERE A KEYNOTE SPEAKER, would you listen to the presenter if he weren't looking directly at you? You wouldn't listen to me. In your mind, you would switch off.

But what happens if this man is engaged in his presentation? What if he was sure about it? He asked the right questions, and he said the things you wanted to say. His man was very talking. You'd like to talk to him.

If you want to close a business deal, you need to express self-confidence to your prospective customer. If you want to be considered for a position, you need to demonstrate self-confidence to the interviewers.

I was accused of having a sense of arrogance when I was interviewed. But I've got the kind of work I've been talking about. An interviewer would prefer to hire a self-confident person over a non-self-confident person.

Self-confidence makes you target for something you're just dreaming about

ARE you waiting for a big break? Does your life feel unreachable? Self-confidence gives you the guts to ask what you want.

I've had the vision to be a project manager. Everybody told me that it was unlikely, and I should stick to what I learned about science. I had the confidence to ask prospective employers for the job of project manager. I got what I was looking for!

You need to be comfortable if you want to live the life of your dreams. If you don't, the blessings of every day will go by you. You're not asking for what you really want. Don't expect people to read your mind about it. Ask for it!

Self-confidence helps you make the right decisions

WHEN YOU ARE SELF-CONFIDENT, you choose to be self-confident. Most of the people who lack self-confidence want to please people. They're not picking themselves. Because they don't, they're making the wrong decisions.

The more you make the right decisions in line with your deepest desires and core values, the faster you achieve your goals.

Self-confidence is what makes you productive

YOU NEED to be productive and manage your time wisely. Eliminate all unnecessary activities. Without self-confidence, you cannot do this successfully.

No self-confidence, you're going to spend time doing things that don't help you achieve your goals.

The surprising thing is that this action was performed unintentionally. You don't think this is what you're doing. I found that when I don't feel confident in my ability to achieve an objective, I'm wasting my time. I'm procrastinating. I do repetitive things like reading my emails instead of concentrating on the creative work I want to do.

When you're positive about your skills, you're super productive.

How To Build Self Confidence In Children

WOULDN'T it be wonderful if we could all raise children with the trust and kindness of Little Orphan Annie? Sure, many kids won't have to be friends and take care of their children, outsmart a cold-hearted orphanage matron, live on the streets, or capture the heart of billionaire "Daddy" War bucks. But all children face many hard knocks, and it's important to equip them with enough confidence not only to endure, but to succeed.

It's a tough time to be a child. The teen suicide epidemic is on the rise. Less than one in five students says they've been bullied. The pressure on children to achieve academic achievement is at an all-time high. That's why it is so important to strengthen your child's self-esteem.

Self-confidence derives from a sense of professionalism. A happy child needs an optimistic, rational view of his or her ability. This is the product of successes, great and small. Your encouraging words can help to build confidence, especially when referring to your child's specific efforts or abilities.

Here are ten tips to help build confidence in your child:

Love your child

THIS SEEMS TRIVIAL, but it's probably the most important thing you can bring to your child. Even if you're
doing it imperfectly, and who isn't? Always have a lot of
love out of it. The child needs to feel welcomed and
valued, beginning with the parents and expanding to
other communities, such as peers, schoolmates, sports
teams, and the public. When you shout or neglect and
make a second parental error, give your child a hug and
tell her you're sorry and you love her. Unconditional
love is building a strong base of confidence.

22

Give praise where praise is due

IT'S important to give your child appreciation and positive feedback because children, especially young children, judge their quality and success by what you feel. But in your appreciation, be realistic. If a child struggles and has no talent for a particular skill, applaud the initiative, but don't celebrate the performance in an unrealistic way. Restore to your baby that it's OK not to be able to do everything perfectly. Tell him that some things take regular work and training, and sometimes it's OK to move on after you've made the best attempt.

23

Help your child to set realistic expectations

ONCE YOUR CHILD STARTS FOOTBALL, it's all right for her to feel that she'll finally be on the Olympic team. But if she can't make a varsity team in high school and still believes she's an Olympic Caliber player, then she needs to focus on more realistic goals. Instruct your child to set reasonable goals to help avoid feelings of failure. If the target is a stretch, explore some of the short-term steps that can be taken along the road.

Model self-love and positive self-talk

YOU HAVE to respect yourself before you can teach your child to love him or herself. You can model this action by encouraging and thanking yourself when you're doing well. Whether you're running a marathon, getting a job promotion and having a successful dinner party, share your achievements with your children. Speak about the skills and talents and resources you need to achieve those goals. In the same talk, you should remind your child of the qualities that he or she has and how they can be built and used.

Teach resilience

NO ONE FAILS at everything all the time. There's going to be losses and defeats, disappointment and suffering. Use these challenges as learning experiences rather than dwelling in incidents as mistakes or disappointments. The old adage, "Try, try, try again," has merit, particularly when teaching children not to give up. But it's also necessary to affirm the child's feelings rather than say, "Well, just cheer up," or, "You shouldn't feel that awful." It helps children learn to trust their feelings and feel comfortable expressing them. Children will learn that failures are a normal part of life and that they can be controlled. If your son is doing a bad study, don't smother him with sympathy and tell him he's not going to be a good writer. Instead, talk about what steps he can take to make things better next time. When he succeeds, he will be proud of his accomplishments.

26

Instilling freedom and fun

KIDS WHO ARE self-confident are willing to try new things without fear of failure. For younger children, you're going to have to supervise from the sidelines. Set up scenarios where she can do something on her own and make sure the situation is safe, but then give her space. For starters, teach how to make a sandwich, and then let her do it on her own, without you hovering or taking part. Encourage discovery, whether it's a visit to a new park or a new dinner. Day trips and activities, new hobbies, holidays or visits with co-workers and school-mates can all widen your child's horizons and build confidence in her ability to deal with new situations.

27

Encourage sports or other
physical activity

NO LONGER THE only domain of boys, sports help girls and boys build trust. They learn that they can practice, improve and achieve their goals. Certain benefits: learn to appreciate their talents, embrace and improve their vulnerabilities, resolve loss, grow their circle of friends, and learn to work together. Another trust-enhancing bonus: they stay fit and learn to respect their bodies. Try to find the physical activity that he or she likes, whether it's singing, martial arts, cycling and walking.

Support their pursuit of a passion

EVERYBODY EXCELS AT SOMETHING, and it's nice when your child learns something like that. As an adult, respect and support the needs of your child even if they are not of concern to you. Praise your kids when they do something in their burgeoning endeavors. If your son's talent plays guitar in a band, encourage his enthusiasm as long as it doesn't compete with commitments like schoolwork. This doesn't mean you give your teenager a free rein to stay out all night or smoke pot in your garage, which brings us to the next tip.

Set the rules and be compliant with them

KIDS ARE MORE relaxed once they know who is in charge and what to expect from them. Even if your child thinks the rules are too rigid, she'll find faith in what she can and can't do when you set and enforce the rules consistently. Each household will have different rules, and they will change over time based on your child's age. Whoever the household rules are, be straightforward about what's important to your parents. Learning and following the rules gives children a sense of security and trust. As children grow older, they may have more input into rules and responsibilities. But it's important to remember that you're not the best friend of yours. You remember, sometimes when your child.

29

Coach relationship skills

RELATIONSHIP CONFIDENCE IS the secret to your child's self-confidence. The most significant initial bond is the parent-child partnership of love. But as your child's social network grows, you'll let her see how her actions affect others and make her grow to retain an inner core of integrity when someone else's actions affect her. As a mother, it's not your job to "fix" any problem, but rather to teach your child empathy, humility, self-assertiveness and, yes, faith in coping with the ups and downs of relationships.

A Paradigm For Self-Love And Positive Self-Talk

YOU HAVE to respect yourself before you can teach your child to love him or herself. You can model this behavior by rewarding and praising yourself when you're doing well. Whether you're running a marathon, getting a job promotion or having a successful dinner party, share your achievements with your children. Speak about the skills and talents and resources you need to achieve those goals. In the same talk, you should remind your child of the qualities that he or she has and how they can be built and used.

30

Understanding Self-Esteem

WE ALL AGREE THAT SELF-ESTEEM, also referred to as self-worth or self-respect, can be an important part of success. People with low self-esteem can feel defeated or be flooded with unnecessary stress, resulting in poor choices being made. Bad choices can lead to negative relationships, reduced job results, and diminished overall health, although it may be risky for someone with low self-esteem. Individuals with high self-esteem levels are also at risk of negative experiences. The problem of self-esteem is how you feel for yourself. How much are you fond of yourself, and what are you worth for yourself? When learning about self-esteem and how to improve the attributes, these are great questions to ask. You will learn not to expect anything less from anyone else when you know more about yourself (especially what makes you feel more confident and how much you deserve for yourself). And if you can do so, you'll build stronger ties with the people around you, put your best foot forward in all you do, and be a much happier person overall.

Self-esteem defines a person's overall sense of self-esteem and personal value. It may involve different assumptions about oneself, such as evaluating one's personality, opinion, attitude, or actions. Often self-esteem is seen as self-image, self-esteem, self-respect, and self-esteem. It can be seen from the point of view of the basic necessity that we have for natural, healthy development, something that emerges from acquired values and beliefs and usually has strong ties to our thought, feelings and actions. Your self-image is how you evaluate your own life, how you feel about your job, your relationships, where you're going in life, and how you see yourself, among other things.

How do you think for yourself? Would you equate yourself favorably with others, or do you appear to be superior/inferior to others? Do you have a rough, negative opinion of yourself? How do you know if your self-esteem is healthy?

Healthy self-esteem is commonly seen as a rational self-esteem: I am equal to others, I have good qualities, I can do things as well as most others, I can be proud of myself, I can be confident with successful people, I can be frank with myself.

A non-realistic self-assessment would fall into the category of pride-I am inferior to others. Thoughts and feelings of inferiority, when weighed against others, will mean a low self-esteem, and inadequate self-esteem. A sign of maturity is the ability to give to others and to meet the needs of others. But we can only offer to others if we have a positive view of ourselves.

Some of the ways to measure self-esteem individually would be:

- You must show yourself properly.
- There is no doubt that others will be denied.

- You must make a final decision about your own well-being.
- You're taking a positive approach towards yourself.
- You can forgive others for making mistakes, and you can forgive yourself.
- You must accept it yourself.
- All in all, you are happy with yourself.
- You know that you have a number of good qualities.
- You can accept criticism with grace.

EFFECTIVE PRACTICES in self-esteem appraisal can be beneficial for personal growth. What the heck are you best at? Make a list of your achievements and personal strengths. How do you see yourself? Write down the positive characteristics and qualities that you have. What do you like to do about it? Schedule time to take action on these issues. Do something new, a sport, a game, a new thing. What do you want to improve about yourself or about your life? Make a few goals and moves to achieve them a little at a time. The person with positive self-worth generally gets more of their needs and wants to be met, and lives a more satisfied and full life!

Self-esteem is the true sense that you have of your own meaning, which is extracted from your impressions, both conscious and unconscious of your beliefs to others. It can be further described as the confidence you have in your ability to perform activities and achieve goals that are considered important. Simply put, self-esteem is like you unconditionally, as you are, regardless of the size of your outfit and physical condition. In my opinion, there are several different types of self-esteem, or should I say levels of self-esteem, which are high, low, middle ground and neutral?

High self-esteem is extremely self-thinking, which in most situations is seen as the basis for career success and good relations with others. When you feel good, this affects the way you think, behave, and feel about others, as well as the goals you accomplish. Now there is a drawback to high self-esteem, and it comes when you equate your worth to another person and decide or consider yourself superior. This almost always results in feelings of pride, selfishness, and difficulties in being with, not healthy!

Low self-esteem, on the other hand, is just the same, when you dwell on your own shortcomings, inadequacies, and other people's perceptions of you, you will be immobilized by self-pity and self-hatred. The more negative you think about yourself, the lower your self-esteem. If you have low self-esteem, you have little faith in your ability, and you doubt your self-esteem, which is the cause of, or I should say, the source of overeating, drinking, drug abuse, marriage loss, physical, psychological, and emotional abuse, and the list goes on.

Low self-esteem, in my opinion, also has several different faces, and I would like to label them as:

- The Pretender
- The Rebel
- The Loser

The Pretender

THE PRETENDER IS an individual who acts successful, happy and content, but in reality they are afraid of failure and fearful someone will find out and reveal them. Individual needs continue to succeed in preserving a shell of positive self-esteem, which usually leads to problems of procrastination, burn-out, rivalry, and perfectionism.

The Rebel

THE REBEL HAS total disregard for the figures of authority and thrives, as well as lives in continuous anger, due to a feeling of not being "good enough" or a "failure." This individual must continually prove that the criticisms, judgments and ridicules do not come to them, which in turn triggers questions of responsibility, blames others for their failures or mistakes, breaks the rules or laws and fights the authority. And this is usually the main reason why the perpetrator was victimized.

33

The Losers

THE LOSERS BEHAVE as if they are unable to cope with life and always need to be saved, powerless and unable to deal with everyday life issues such as household chores, shopping visits, fuel buying, just to name a few. The person uses ignorance and self-pity as a defense for fear of taking responsibility for improving his or her life. This type of individual constantly relies on others for direction and guidance, which leads the individual to under-achievement, lack of assertiveness and over-reliance on others in relationships.

Overall, the consequences of low self-esteem can be devastating, ranging from anxiety to stress and loneliness. Low self-esteem leads to struggles with violence, and has a devastating effect on friendships, marriages, and can severely affect educational and work results. It can lead to underachievement and increase the suscepti-bility of sexual addiction, substance use and alcohol abuse.

Worst of all, these negative consequences themselves perpetuate the negative self-image and can drive an individual to a downward spiral of lower and lower self-esteem and increasingly unproductive or even violent self-destructive behavior.

Getting a self-esteem that is too high or too low should be impossible, because there is always a middle ground, and even if it can be volatile, you'll feel like you're on a roller coaster that oscillates between feeling good about you and feeling bad about you. Feeling good, or I should refer to them as successors, increasing your self-esteem and feeling bad, tends to keep you on an even thus acknowledging the presence of good, thereby improving one's ability and setting limits. Not everyone has the composite to hit the middle ground, and we need to abandon all criticism of themselves and others and just go in neutral while knowing that they cannot judge themselves or others specifically.

Healthy self-esteem is based on the individual's ability to judge himself or herself when accepting, and to evaluate himself or herself unconditionally. That essentially means to be truthful in your acknowledgment of your shortcomings, flaws, talents, and successes, while at the same time accepting yourself as capable, significant, and it's worth it without reservations, precautions or conditions. Lives are far too complicated, and they are too prevalent for an individual to create more problems, problems, and negative emotions through a lack of self-esteem. Low or I should say that unhealthy self-esteem is going to block you from seeing the forest for the trees, knowing that in most cases, what you think about yourself and others really doesn't have any meaning anyway, it's nothing but a temporary feeling, if that's it. My goal is to be selfless and non-judgmental when living life to the fullest. What really matters is a pure, clear understanding of what you really are in the hands of the creator, not in the eyes of man, in other words, focusing on the spiritual side of you to maintain a healthy balance, emotionally and psychologically.

HERE ARE Some Signs Of A High Self-Esteem

- You are able to say' no.'
- You've got a positive attitude.
- You accept the strengths and weaknesses of your own.
- Negative experiences do not have an enormous impact.
- You should share your desires and your emotions.

HERE ARE Signs Of Low Self-Esteem

- You've got a negative mentality.
- You're losing confidence.
- The emphasis is on the negative aspects of life at all times.
- You feel ashamed, sad, and frightened.
- You think other people are better than you.
- You're feeling resentment and envy.
- Compliments cannot be ignored and you are open to any kind of suggestions.
- You're afraid of failure, so you're a perfectionist.

CONFIDENCE IS one of the main aspects of self-esteem training and growth. Self-esteem is about self-love, and getting too much can make you look vain, lazy, insecure, and even arrogant. Not enough self-esteem can make someone accept less than they deserve and carry on too much for their level of stress. That's what we'd call a pushover. The right amount of self-esteem will benefit greatly from how you function, how you see the world, how you communicate with others, and how you handle yourself. One of the many things you can do to develop your self-esteem is to take care of yourself. You look good when you feel good, and do great things.

Self-Esteem In Children

SOMETIMES, it's easy to notice when kids seem to feel good for themselves and when they don't. The concept of feeling good about oneself is often described as "self-esteem."

CHILDREN WITH SELF-ESTEEM:

- Feel loved and welcomed.
- Feel confident.
- Feel proud of what they can do.
- Believe good things about themselves.
- Believe in themselves.

CHILDREN WITH LOW SELF-ESTEEM:

- Are self-critical and harsh on themselves.
- To believe that they're not as good as other kids.

- Think of the times they fail rather than when they succeed.
- Lack of confidence.
- Doubt that they can do something right.

Why Self-Esteem Matters In Children

KIDS WHO FEEL good about themselves have the confidence to try new things. They're most likely to try their hardest. They're proud of what they can do. Self-esteem helps children to deal with mistakes. This helps children try again, even if they fail at first. As a result, self-esteem helps children do better at school, at home, and with peers.

Kids with low self-esteem feel unsure of themselves. If they don't believe others will welcome them, they can't join. They can encourage others to treat them badly. We might have a hard time standing up for themselves. They might give up easily, or they might not try at all. Children with low self-esteem find it hard to deal with when they make a mistake, lose, and fail. As a result, they will not do as well as they might.

How Self-Esteem Develops In Children

WHEN CHILDREN GROW UP, self-esteem can also rise. Any time children try things, do stuff, and learn lessons can be an opportunity for self-esteem to develop. This can happen when the children:

- Making progress towards a target.
- Doing things at school.
- Making friends and learn talents.
- Learn music, athletics, painting, baking, tech skills.
- Improve fun tasks support, share.
- Be kind to get recognition for good behaviors.
- Hard to do something they're good at.
- Are included by others.
- Feel understood and welcomed to get a reward or a better grade they think they've won.

SELF-ESTEEM MAY START as early as childhood. It's evolving slowly over time. It can start because the child feels secure, loved, and welcomed. It can start when a child receives positive attention and loving care.

When babies are teenagers or young children, they can do some stuff on their own. We feel good about themselves when we can make use of their new skills. Their self-esteem grows when the parents pay attention, let the child try, smile, and show their pride.

How Parents May Develop Self-Esteem In Their Children

EACH CHILD IS DIFFERENT. Self-esteem may be better for some children than others. And some kids are faced with issues that can decrease their self-esteem. But even if the child's self-esteem is small, it may be increased.

HERE ARE some things that parents can do to help children feel good about themselves:

Help your child learn how to do things

THERE ARE new things for children to learn at every age. Even during childhood, learning to hold a cup and take the first steps sparks a sense of superiority and joy. When your child grows up, events like learning to dress, read, and ride a bike are a chance for self-esteem to grow.

When you teach kids how to do something

TELL them and motivate them first. Let them do what they can, even if they make mistakes. Make sure your child has a chance to learn, try to feel proud. Don't make new tasks too straightforward or too challenging.

37

Praise your child but do this
wisely

OF COURSE, it's a good thing to compliment kids. Your
praise is a way to show that you are proud of yourself.
But in fact, some ways of praising children can backfire.

Here's how to do the right thing

DON'T EXAGGERATE!

Praise that doesn't sound deserved doesn't really ring true. For example, convincing a child he's played a great game because he realizes he doesn't feel hollow or false. It's better to say, "I know it wasn't your best game, but we've all had a few days off. I'm proud of you for not giving up." Add a vote of confidence: "Tomorrow, you'll be back in your game."

Praise for the initiative

STOP RELYING on outcomes only (such as having an A) or predetermined attributes (such as being intelligent and athletic).

Alternatively, give most of your support for your initiative, success, and attitude. For example, "You're working hard on the task," "You're getting better and better at these spelling tests," and, "I'm proud of you for learning the piano you're still sticking with it." With this kind of affirmation, kids are making progress, striving on objectives, and attempting. If they do that, they are more likely to succeed.

40

Be a good role model for you

YOU'RE SETTING a good example when you put your energy into everyday tasks (such as raking leaves, making a meal, cleaning dishes, and washing a car). Your child learns to make an effort to do homework, to clean up things, or to make a bed.

Modeling the right attitude is also critical. When you do things cheerfully (or at least without grumbling or complaining), you teach your child to do the same thing. If you stop running through tasks and take pride in a job well done, teach your child to do that, too.

Limit the harsh criticisms

THE MESSAGES CHILDREN receive about themselves from others easily translate into how they feel about themselves. Harsh words ("You are so lazy!") are negative, not inspiring. If children hear negative messages about themselves, it affects their self-esteem. Right kids with caution. Reflect on what you want them to do next. Tell them how when they're needed.

42

Focus on your strengths

PAY attention to and enjoy what your child is doing well. Make sure your child has the chance to develop these abilities. Focus more on strengths than shortcomings if you want to help children feel good about themselves. This also changes conduct.

Let the children give and support

SELF-ESTEEM INCREASES as children know that what they do is valuable to others. Kids can help out at home, do a school service project, or do a favor to a friend. Helping and kind behavior to develop self-esteem and other good feelings.

Why Self-Esteem Is Based On A Child's Personal Belief System

IT'S a combination of how children feel about themselves and how people think they see them. Children's sense of self affects their perceptions about what they can do, how to deal with problems, and how to get along with peers. Academic success increases self-confidence and makes the child feel confident. Success in scholastic endeavors also leads to self-doubt. When children have low esteem, they can shy away from new activities and responsibilities, or waste excessive time on personal concerns instead of concentrating on training.

The cornerstone of self-esteem is laid early in children's lives as they build relationships to loving people who respond affectionately to them. If children feel the important others in their life love them, want them to be healthy, and would miss them if they were gone, they are more likely to develop self-esteem. When children are treated with dignity, motivated to do their best, received constructive guidance, provided with direction, and granted chances to influence some of their lives, their self-esteem typically thrives.

Conversely, when children feel unrecognized or incapable of love, a poor self-conception can result. Additional factors that may lead to a low self-esteem include irregular appearance, poor coordination, learning difficulties, attention problems, difficulty with adjustment, race, deprivation and prejudice. Kids don't gain self-esteem from people, showing them how good they are. Alternatively, we develop self-confidence by being known and completing challenging tasks. Praise is important when it is accurate and provides meaningful feedback. It is not necessary to use flattery.

Another factor is that children neither develop self-esteem at once nor are they consistent over time. Both kids are feeling psychological ups and downs. For example, a child can feel self-assured at home, but not in school or in groups. Providing a variety of social and learning opportunities helps to increase the morale of the child.

44

Understanding The Potential Of Positivity

LEARNING how to be more positive and have greater self-esteem than you do has a number of advantageous aspects and can help you excel and live a fulfilling life. Before learning and understanding the influence of positivity, none of this is possible. It can be difficult for most people to cultivate positivity because in many cases we are always trying to control our circumstances and over-think. Many people have low self-esteem, and when they feel too bad for themselves, it's hard to think optimistic. Another explanation of why it can be difficult to obtain positive thinking is that we want something to happen and are often surprised by the consequences, if not what we expected. It reverses our thinking and encourages us to think about most things in our lives in a negative way. So positive thinking, though, is not about seeing the best in everything, but simply embracing the negative as a way of life with the better.

So what exactly is positivity definition? It's not what you're, but something you're doing. For a while, psychologists have been researching the power of positive thinking and found that positive thinking can rewrite the pain that you have endured. Positive thinking will allow you to change pessimistic patterns of thinking because researchers today show that the more you practice using a positive mind, the happier you will become. It indicates that positive thinking is an innate skill, not something you were born with and automatically knew how to do it.

Positive thinking is perhaps one of the easiest things to do; however, our brain would automatically look for the negatives based on the experiences of an individual. Positive thinking is tougher than most would like to say.

Below are a few ways you can incorporate positivity in your life:

45

Take heed and be conscious

MINDFULNESS HAS BEEN around for years, creating deeper neural connections, helping people to be more innovative, remembering better memories, making better decisions, and keeping you calmer overall.

You need to learn to do the following to gain awareness:

- Track your emotions and surroundings; do not mark as good or bad any feeling or experience. Only be with them, then. Observe them and be on them without prejudice.
- Perform one thing at a time rather than trying multitasking. If you're having a conversation, for example, just have the conversation. Effectively listen without instantly answering. Give yourself time to consider and then be successful in answering. Put away the phone and any other threats and concentrate on just one thing.
- For at least five (better ten) minutes each day, be alone with yourself. This is the moment

when you're doing almost nothing, just listening and keeping in mind what's going on inside and around you. No phone, no books, no tv, no music, just you and your thoughts.

Be appreciative

MANY PEOPLE HAVE such busy lives that they forget about the little stuff they've brought to where they're. Pay attention to the things you're thankful for, small and big. Here are some reminders of what to be grateful for: you have been waking today.

- You have a loving and caring family.
- You have a nice warm cup of tea to drink.
- You have to take a shower of hot water.
- You have to look forward to things.

Begin Small

SINCE POSITIVITY IS something you're doing and you're practicing from (you're not), you've got to start small. It occurs when you become conscious that you will be able to catch the positive moments in your life. Has anybody been making dinner today? Have you been fucking up and feeling bad about it at work? And take advantage of these chances to be optimistic. You will begin to see more positivity slowly and overtime and then naturally get it.

Improve The Life Sometimes

WE ARE SURROUNDED by negativity in our office, home, marriages, etc. While it is important to look for positivity in your life, if negativity is unbearable, you should also know how to change your surroundings. Here are some things you can do to turn the negative environment into a positive one.

- Hang out with those who value you and your values and positive people.
- Try new things, such as meeting a book club at the local food bank and volunteering.
- Write motivational and encouraging online articles.
- Take sticky notes with positive statements and phrases everywhere.
- Have a good friend. For example, if your friend tries to be more optimistic, call them at the end of the day every day to talk about all the good things you've done and talked about today.

49

Journal

JOURNALING IS one of the best things you can do if you go through a difficult time and find it tough to be motivated. Journaling helps you to write down what your worries are, and look at what you've read from the viewpoint of a third person. You will be able to see the positive through the negatives by journaling, because the feelings are now placed on paper rather than spinning around in your mind. Many people only use newspapers for pressure and negative thinking. Others have articles on preparation and scheduling. And some others are newspapers with positivity. Figure out what kind of journaling is right for you and make it a routine every day.

Every day, you will rebalance your life by taking small steps towards positivity and rewire your mind to look at the brighter side of everything. Feeling positive is not about being happy and fulfilled; when you can't control it, it's more about learning how to be optimistic despite tough times and being cynical.

PERSONALITY AND SELF-WORTH

Personality and self-worth

SELF-WORTH IS DEFINED as a person who, as an entity, senses their own importance or quality. A person may respect himself and evaluate his or her worth as an entity in multiple ways. While self-esteem is the same in some way as self-esteem, in fact, the two are quite different from each other. Self-worth is more about valuing your own beliefs and morals as a human than judging yourself on the basis of your actions. In short, self-esteem is about who you are, not what you are doing, while self-esteem is based on what you are doing. In other words, self-esteem is quite the reverse in this way. Nevertheless, there are many differences in expressing self-esteem and self-worth. High self-esteem is dependent on contrasting oneself with others, but self-esteem is based solely on how a person sees himself without the judgment of anyone else, which shows high levels of self-confidence in another way.

The first step in increasing and enhancing your self-worth is to stop comparing with others and setting high self-esteem goals. That internal critical voice is the only thing that stands in the way of enhancing that self-worth. In the way you think, the inner critic plays a big part. Your vital inner voice gets in the way if you feel badly. Positive thinking can trump those nasty negative thoughts and monitor them. The first step in addressing the negative thoughts in our heads who tell us we can't do anything is to consider ourselves at a deeper level and get to know ourselves fully. We should foster self-esteem and practice self-compassion. The next step in being deserving is kind to ourselves. Below are the three steps of self-compassion:

- To consider and acknowledge the pain and suffering.
- Be kind to yourself and take care of your own pain.
- Note that imperfection and errors are common to us all, and in order for personal growth, these things need to happen.

IT WILL GIVE you an immense mental and physical boost in self-worth to support others and to be kind to others. So, if you want or can offer a lunch to the hungry, donate. Eventually, you can monitor and deal with your inner detractors by being kind to yourself through healthy habits and mental exercises, thereby creating self-worth. Do new things and enjoy events that support your personal convictions. You will grow and improve your own self-worth by doing so.

What Is Caring For Oneself?

SELF-LOVE IS when you know when and how to take care of yourself because you know that you need to be cared for within your self-worth. Who is better than you to take care of you? Some people may think that self-love means having arrogant traits or becoming excessively greedy about getting what you want and need. In reality, the opposite is very much. Self-love means acknowledging your flaws and appreciating everything you are. In other words, it's the desire to value yourself despite mistakes and deficiencies. So how do you take care of yourself and admit all your own mistakes? By empathy for oneself. The way to do this is to look at yourself as if you're a relative or someone you respect, and tell yourself how you're going to treat them. Whatever the response is, it's just how you must handle yourself. Loving yourself is offering yourself what it takes for your heart, body, and soul to nourish and develop into the person you want to be.

Many people think you're giving yourself attention by buying new clothes and hearing inspirational quotes or even engaging with someone who makes you feel good. It's not that. These are only quick solutions, and if the goal is to enjoy yourself more, they will not help you in the long run. That's why. Having new clothes gives us a sense of pride but not love (especially if we worked hard for them). Writing motivational papers gives us a sense of fulfillment, but for a short time only. The reason we get attention from other people is to get involved in a relationship that makes us feel good and valued. The phase of the honeymoon will end, though, and then the hard part of the marriage will happen. If you don't learn to love yourself, it will be more difficult to resolve arguments and disputes. Self-love is more than just feeling good by materialistic things and self-fulfillment. It's about being truly supported through acts that help and improve your mental, religious, and physical development.

You can do some stuff to practice self-love:

Stay aware

JUST LIKE PRACTICING POSITIVITY AWARENESS, while trying to develop self-love, you can also exercise compassion. For just about anything, you should consider being conscious. But when you begin your observance meditation or mindfulness techniques, make sure you know what your goal is, which will help you get closer to your target. To be inspired by long-term stimulation and mindfulness, you need to learn every day to cultivate awareness and devote yourself to it before you begin to see real effects.

Find out what you need and forget what you want

TO ENJOY yourself is to give yourself what you need instead of doing what you need. For us, our urges are dangerous most of the time. Of starters, if we want to binge-drink and party for a couple of days because when we do this we feel better, we actually damage our bodies. Or if you have a shopping addiction and go to the dollar store and clothing store and end up wasting money on things you don't need, you're actually training your mind that impulses are more important than other important things, such as food or savings. You could have time for yourself, like taking a long shower, listening to relaxing music, or doing something about yourself that you haven't done in a while, instead of partying for a couple of days. You can save for a nice new home and develop up reputation so you can have financial security with the money you spend buying stuff which ends up getting misplaced and given away.

53

Paying attention to oneself

INDIVIDUALS WHO THINK about themselves know what they need. We know that short-term "exciting" things, in the long run, will only make them feel good and evil. This is the time to feed on healthy activities such as exercising, eating right, sleeping properly, and relationships of confidence.

Set restrictions

YOU WILL ALSO DEVELOP self-discipline and do what you need to do for yourself. You teach yourself limits if you show high performance at work, say no to drama, don't indulge in unhealthy relationships, and deplete negative behaviors. Self-love comes easily from setting boundaries, and you'll know how to value yourself more.

55

Pardon yourself

EVERYONE IS MAKING MISTAKES. Often we dive into bad choices that we know will not turn right. We set such high expectations for ourselves, and when we are not good, we blame ourselves. Often, even when we know it's not our fault, we blame ourselves when things go wrong. You need to forgive yourself and be careful with who you are in order to defeat this cycle. Learn to accept your faults, reflect on your shortcomings, but above all, appreciate the person you are because you deserve it.

Focus on one of these at a time, and you will finally find it throughout the entire list. It's not a complete list of how to treat yourself, but it's a start and a step in the right direction.

What Is Self-Respect?

MOST PEOPLE that do not have self-respect are looking to please everyone, and usually, they have a hard time saying no. Having respect for yourself means that you know deep down that you are worthy of being treated fairly and with respect. If you are someone who seems to attract the type of people who mistreat you or if you seem to be attracted to narcissists, then you probably don't have much respect for yourself, and oftentimes, you may not even realize that you lack self-respect. However, if you don't learn how to respect yourself now, then you are more than likely going to follow the same patterns, settling for less and struggling to find your voice. You are likely to make too many commitments and let other people walk all over you. Having self-respect ensures that boundaries are solidly in place so that you are treated well and fairly in all aspects. You have to ensure that your needs and desires are met, and your voice is heard.

It helps to understand what it takes to have self-respect so that you can try to develop the trait for your own personal growth. Below are some characteristics of people who have self-respect:

- Being assertive.
- Having no toleration for people who mistreat them or talk down to them.
- Not associating with unreliable people who walk all over them.
- Having strong boundaries in place for the people who try to take advantage of them and suck their energy.
- Being able to say no to unreasonable requests and not feeling guilty or pressured to say yes because they know what is good and what is unhealthy.
- Having clear values and boundaries in a relationship, such as no lying.
- Knowing the worth of their work.
- No settling for less than they deserve in any situation.

DO YOU SEE A PATTERN? Living your life with the utmost respect for yourself shows that you are committed and comfortable in every aspect of your life, which is safe and necessary. There are many advantages of having self-respect and confidence and understanding what you deserve. Some of them are as follows:

- You respect and honor your needs and desires.
- You have more time for yourself to do stuff and work for your goals.

- You feel equal, not above or below, to others.
- You have better friends and friendships that last longer.
- Your professional success and reliability are valued.
- You find in death a sense of fulfillment.
- You feel trustworthy and deserving.
- For yourself and others, you have a deeper understanding of faith.
- You more closely follow your intuitions.

THIS IS NOT a complete list of the benefits of self-respect; nevertheless, having self-respect means enabling yourself to fulfill your dreams and reach your long-term goals. This is because you know what you want and are committed to what you think you deserve.

Self-respect is also about the dignity of yourself and the reality of who you are. Because when you honor yourself and your truth, you can honor all people by treating them with dignity, love and respect that we all need and deserve.

How To Respect Yourself

DEVELOPING a strong sense of self-respect will help you realize your abilities, develop healthy relationships, and make everyone around you see you as a person worthy of respect. If you really want to honor yourself, then you have to embrace yourself and aspire to become the person you've always dreamed of becoming. Take steps to learn how to feel happy about who you are and make the world treat you like you deserve to be treated.

Below are tangible ways to understand yourself.

Getting In The Right Mindset

GET TO KNOW YOURSELF!

The more you know yourself, the more you will see and recognize how special you really are, and the more you will love yourself. Explore your values, your character, and your strengths. It may take a while to complete this exciting process of self-discovery, but you'll quickly see that it was worth it.

Make a list of things, friends, emotions and experiences that matter to you. This list will help you identify what you really like and need for your life.

Try different things. It gives you a chance to see what you like and what you don't like.

Try writing in a notebook. Pretend that you're speaking to your 99-year-old self and asking for advice on what to work on in your life. You can also start writing a question, "What do I want to avoid writing about?" This will initiate an honest conversation about yourself.

Spend time with yourself and thinking that you're dating yourself. Try a new restaurant that's just what you'd like to do.

This is going to give you a great chance to connect with your own feelings and opinions.

Forgive yourself

IF YOU WANT to respect yourself, then you must be able to forgive yourself for the things you have done in the past that you are not proud of. Admit what you did was wrong, apologize to others, if necessary, and try to move on. If you're too harsh on yourself to make the wrong decision and do anything hurtful, then you're never going to be able to move on. Know that you're alive. People are making mistakes. Making errors is the way we learn, but embrace them and forgive yourself.

Embrace yourself

BE comfortable in your own skin, learn to love and embrace the person you are. This doesn't mean you have to think you're perfect, but you have to learn to embrace yourself. Be pleased with all the things you love about yourself, and be okay with those pieces of you that are less than ideal, particularly those that you can't change.

Stop telling me you're going to love yourself if you just lose 20 pounds, and start loving the woman you're right here right now.

Work on building your confidence

IT'S hard to achieve self-respect if you're not pleased with who you are, what you feel, or what you do. Building true trust takes a lot of work, but doing a few simple things every day can start you on your way.

Start by maintaining a positive body language and a good posture, smiling more and thinking at least three good thoughts about yourself every hour.

If someone compliments you, accept their point, saying, "Thank you."

Keep a positive outlook

A POSITIVE ATTITUDE can make or break your life's success, as well as your thoughts about who you are. Even if things don't go your way, be sure that something positive is bound to happen. Be happy with your everyday life and all that it has to offer you. When you feel overly cynical about everything and just foresee the worst in any situation, then you're likely never to feel good about who you are and give yourself the respect you deserve.

For example, when you applied for a job that you really want, don't think, "There's no way I'll get it. There are so many more qualified applicants. "Instead, say," It would be so exciting to get the job done. Even if I'm not called for an interview, I'm still proud of myself.

Stop trying to keep up with everyone

ONE OF THE reasons you may lack self-respect is that you feel bad that you're single while all your friends are married, or that you feel inadequate that you don't make as much money as other people you know. Maintain your own values and work to achieve the targets you want to reach. Don't waste your time doing what you think would annoy your Facebook friends and give you the right to brag. It's a lot more impressive to excel in doing what you want to do instead of following the path that everyone else has followed.

64

Put aside your jealousy

STOP WISHING you had what someone had to do and work to achieve what you really want. Feelings of bitterness and resentment that come with jealousy will only make you dislike yourself and wish you were someone else. Cast aside envy and work on what makes you happy.

65

Trust in your decisions

IF YOU WANT to honor yourself, you have to trust in the choices you have made. You have to be firm in your convictions and make an effort to understand yourself and to know what is going to make you happy. Allow yourself the satisfaction of a well-made decision and stick to it, no matter how difficult it may be.

It's all right to ask other people for advice, and this can actually help you develop a more balanced perspective, but you shouldn't spend your time doubting yourself, worrying that what you've done is all wrong, or believing you've done something else.

Learn how to deal with criticism

TO REALLY HAVE SELF-RESPECT, you need to be aware of the person you really are. If someone gives you helpful and constructive input, remember what they're asking you. You may be able to use suggestions to better yourself. Constructive criticism will help you achieve the goal of becoming a better person.

Your husband could suggest that you could have been a better listener when he really needed you, or your employer could say that your study might have been prepared more carefully, If someone is rude and trying to hurt you, chuck the criticism out of the window. Sometimes it can be hard to tell the difference between someone who tells you something that's real in a tough way and someone who tells you something that's "good" to say. Evaluate these observations frankly and deliberately.

Don't let others get to you

ALTHOUGH IT MAY SOUND IMPOSSIBLE, your sense of self-worth and happiness should come from yourself, not from the people around you. Yes, any praise and bonuses can make you feel better, but at the end of the day, the joy and self-satisfaction will come from within. Don't let anyone ask you who you are, make you feel low, or make you question your values. If you want to love yourself, you have to believe that you have made the right decisions and learn to let the haters hate you.

If you always let people change your mind and make you rethink your choices, people will think you don't have strong convictions. Once you find things that you really believe in, it's going to be harder to let all the negative people in your life get to you.

68

Taking Action With Yourself

TREAT YOURSELF WITH DIGNITY!
We often do things to ourselves that we never dream of doing to those we care for. For e.g., when you last called a hideous buddy, told them they weren't good enough, or stopped them from following their dreams? Everything you consider to be fair, add it to yourself. Do not offend or hurt yourself, no matter how bad you think. This kind of therapy is bound to make you feel better. Here are some other ways to handle yourself with intrinsic respect:
Don't steal from yourself!

- By imprudently putting everything on credit, you're basically taking cash from your future self, and ultimately you're going to have to pay.
- Be frank to yourself instead of being in doubt about what you really want to do.
- Think for yourself by creating your own information sources and doing research, instead of just pursuing the views of others.

Take care of your body

WHEN YOU MAKE an effort to keep your body in good working order, not only will you feel better physically, but you will also feel a sense of pride. Respecting the body always means not judging it for what it is, of course. Make an effort to get healthier and stay healthy, but don't think about things you can't control, like your ratios. Focus on things that you can change and improve, and do it because you feel good, not because you don't believe you're "great enough" the way you are. This doesn't mean that going to the gym and looking amazing would automatically lead you to a high level of self-respect. But it does mean that if you don't invest much time or care into your look, you'll begin to lose regard for who you are.

Target areas for improvement

RESPECTING yourself does not mean thinking that you are fine and that there is absolutely nothing you need to focus on and build on. It means being able to accept things that you can't change about yourself while working on things that you need to work on. Take some time to really think about yourself and consider the areas where you'd like to work most; maybe you'd like to improve your listening skills, or you'd love to do a lot better with your little daily stress, or you'd like to have a more balanced approach to making people around you happy without sacrificing your own needs.

- Make a plan to make some progress in these areas, and then you'll be on your way to being more accepting of yourself. Make a list of things that you would like to change. Take note if you make any changes, however, limited they may be. It's important to write down your small and great victories.
- Of note, altering habits and the thoughts and feelings associated with these activities take

more than a day or two; this takes a great deal of effort and patience. Yet taking the first steps to becoming a more respected person would make you feel more comfortable about who you are.

Improve yourself

IMPROVING yourself means taking steps to try new things and open your mind to new possibilities.

Improving yourself can mean taking a yoga class, fundraising, spending more time learning lessons from the people you care for, learning to see multiple perspectives on the issue, reading news, or trying to learn new things.

Interacting With Others

RESPECT PEOPLE!

If you want to honor yourself, then you have to start by loving the people around you, not just the ones who have more experience or are more advanced, but all the human beings on this planet who have not hurt you. For example, many people don't deserve your respect, but you should try and treat people like you want to be handled, whether you're speaking to your boss or a check-out woman in your local grocery store. Here are some simple ways to value others:

- To be honest with people.
- Don't rob, hurt, or offend them.
- Listen to what they say, respect their thoughts, and stop interrupting them.

Recognize when people disrespect you and take steps to stop it

A PERSON with self-respect does not encourage others to treat them poorly, and would prefer not to interact with someone who is arrogant. This may seem simple, but there are many occasions where we tolerate being treated badly (both in big and small ways) because we think the person doesn't know better, or because we're not ready to let that person go, or because we're too down on ourselves to feel that we deserve better. If someone doesn't give you basic respect, stand up for yourself, and tell that person to treat you differently.

If someone is always disrespecting you, let him go. Nobody said it was easy to turn your back on someone who obviously disrespected you, when you care a lot about that man. But once you break the bad habit of associating with someone who makes you feel terrible, you're going to feel your self-respect.

Know how to recognize a coercive and manipulating friendship. It can be difficult to see if a person close to us is rude, particularly if they're sly or sneaky, and it's been going on for a long time.

73

Learn to practice non-violent communication

IF YOU QUESTION someone about their disrespectful behavior, try to stick to the positive and productive interpersonal guidelines: don't scream or offend the other person. These types of actions are at the heart of the discourse in judgment and are not successful.

- Identify your emotions, please.
- Be frank about what you feel about taking responsibility for these feelings.
- Clearly, state what you need or want from this situation.
- You might think, "I need a better picture of myself, and I don't want to listen to negative comments about myself."

Don't focus too much on others to make you feel good

Many times, in dating or relationships, we may neglect our own desires and allow ourselves to be dominated by others because we are too afraid to lose them. You might see their views matter a lot more than your own. In fact, paying attention to everyone else's desires, but yours is a typical sign of low self-respect. Alternatively, trust your own instincts and put your interests first. Know that for your fulfillment. You don't need to rely on someone else.

A good place to start with is to find out what you can control and what you can't control. Of starters, you can't control other people's actions (you can affect them, but you can't control them), and you can't control the weather. But even in bad situations, you can control how you respond to strangers, and you can control how you choose to behave.

You can also take action to improve the management of different relationship situations, such as learning to be more assertive, and learning about healthy boundaries, how to implement them, and how to adhere to them. This will help you learn positive behavior patterns that will inspire people to treat you well and increase self-respect.

74

Forgive others

IF YOU WANT to honor yourself, you have to learn to forgive the ones who have wronged you. This doesn't mean that you have to be the best friends to them, but it does mean that you have to forgive them for learning to move on emotionally. When you spend all your time worrying about all your grudges and resentments, otherwise you won't be able to think clearly and live in the present. Now, do yourself the favor of pardoning criminals so that you can move on.

Even if someone has caused you unspeakable harm, you need to focus on moving on from the experience and the man. You can't let yourself wallow in anger and resentment forever.

Forgiving others is a favor which you owe yourself, and an activity that you do for your own self-healing. It's all right to be angry for a little while, but if you're angry for too long, the rage will mess with your life and happiness. Realize that when people treat you poorly, it's because they're not treating people well in their life, so they might be worse off than you. So forgive them for their own errors and transgressions, and the one who will profit the most is you.

Being Good For Yourself

DON'T DEMEAN YOURSELF!

If you want to honor yourself, you must stop demeaning yourself, particularly in front of others. It's one thing to chuckle at yourself, but it's another thing to say something like, "I feel too fat today," and, "Why would anyone want to speak to me anyway?" When you put yourself down, you allow others to do the same thing.[13] The next time you think poorly about yourself, write it down instead of saying it aloud. When you say it out loud, you're more likely to believe it's real.

Don't let other people see you do something you'll regret later

TRY to focus on doing things that make you proud of yourself, not just things that get cheap laughs and short-term publicity. Stay away from regretful actions, such as getting too drunk or being messy in public, and hooking up with someone at a bar just for your money.

Try to keep a clear picture of yourself. It's going to be hard for people to respect you as the smartest guy in school when you bounced around with a lampshade on your face at a party the night before.

Dealing with powerful emotions

IT'S all right to lose your coolness from time to time, but if you lose your coolness too often and over the small stuff, it will improve your self-respect to cope more easily with the little stress of life. Take a jog to cool down, take deep breaths, and get back to the situation when you're calmer. Dealing with life's problems with a calm mind rather than with high emotions will make you feel more in control and happier about how you approach your everyday situations, which, in effect, will increase your self-respect.

If you feel angry, excuse yourself and go for a short walk, get some fresh air, and contact someone who can help you feel grounded. You can also try meditation, read in a book, or speak to someone else.

Admit it when you're wrong

IF YOU REALLY WANT TO HONOR YOURSELF, then you need to know when you've made a mistake. If you've messed up, let people know in a way that shows you're truly sorry and that you've given ample attention to the situation to stop doing the same thing again in the future. Taking responsibility for what you do and trying your best to make amends for it will help you move beyond feeling bad about making a mistake that will boost your self-respect, because you will realize and be proud of the fact that you did your best, even though things didn't go as well as you would have liked. Allow yourself and the people around you enough dignity to be able to admit that you are only human.

When you learn to admit that you're right, people will have a lot more respect for you and more faith in you.

Spend your time with the people who admire you

LIVING around people who make you feel worse for

yourself is likely to lower your self-respect, because you will feel bad not only because of what that person says, but deep down, you will also be angry at yourself for letting that person stick around you. Choose people who make you feel positive, better about yourself and the world, and who actually take the time to listen to you and help you work out your feelings. This is especially true of relationships. It'll be almost difficult to have true self-respect if you're dating someone who makes you feel useless.

Stay humble

MANY PEOPLE THINK that lying about their successes would make people more like them. Doing this, though, will potentially make you look dangerous. If you really want people to respect you, show modesty and dignity, let other people know for themselves how amazing you are.

What Is Self-Criticism?

A SELF-CRITIC IS a person whose feelings about every-thing they do are uncontrollable and sometimes distract-ing. You may define a self-critic as an over-thinker or someone with an unconscious negative thinking habit in their mind. Even if you seek to be optimistic, your inner critic could say things like "You're not going to get the job" or "Why can't you do it right?" The inner critic's habit is the nagging" voices "or feelings that form an internalized conversation of discontent and self-doubt. The critical voice is the one questioning each of our actions. This influences almost every aspect of our lives, causing us to feel powerless and less self-confident. Negative thoughts are more important than we know of ourselves. It can build self-doubt, encourage mistrust, lead to self-denial, blame for addictions and drug use, and, worst of all, facilitate mental illness.

The reason critical thought or the inner critic's voice is so strong for most people is because it derives from past experiences. The thought process is already estab-lished in the brain before someone knows it, which is why so many of us get stressed out so quickly. Many people don't realize that their internal critics are having such an immense effect on their lives, so to overcome the inner critics you need to be mindful of when it happens. Once you are aware of what the negative thought means and can identify exactly, you can start questioning it by talking about the whole idea. You must knowingly take the steps needed to let the idea go intentionally. When consciously replacing the negative thought with a positive, take control of yourself. The key is not pushing away your feelings, but being with them. Track them and then let them vanish by themselves without paying attention to them or naming them. Getting aware of this technique is named.

You will start to find the causes once you are fully aware of the voice of your inner critic. Triggers occur when something has been done to trigger your subconscious anger. The next thing to do when you find your triggers is to reframe your outlook on your triggers. You're going to a friend's house, for example, and at first, you're talking about how happy you're to see them. Once you leave, though, you start to ask yourself why you've been there. Why are you holding this friend in your life when they don't need you in reality? They're being good to you because they're sorry. If this one friend just happens, you need to reframe your thinking and find out exactly why you're keeping this buddy around. Find the true intentions of them. Spend more time with them to show to your mind that you have no risk in your life with this guy. You have exercised self-respect and self-love when they turn out to be genuine. When they turn out to be really good, maybe the inner opponent has just been reframed. In spite of your feelings, the trick is not to ignore the triggers but to dive deeper into your triggers so that they no doubt become a threat.

To overcome the inner critic, here are just a few simple steps:

Focus on the task at hand and avoid over-thinking

IF YOU GET STUCK TOO much in your own head, that's when self-criticism is going to happen. If you had a project at home and you didn't do as well as you would have wanted, working on it will just make you doubt your own ability.

Reflect on what's in front of you, and put aside all the other distractions for a while. When I have a plan or an important task with an uncompromising timetable, there is a little space for over-thinking and doubting, the work needs to be done. I'm taking a piece of paper and I'm splitting the job into a little bit of to-do list of moves to get me on the right track like bread crumbles to guide the way. This keeps me focused all the time on what's in front of me.

Take a walk and breathe deeply

AFTER A POOR MEETING OR SPEECH, it's easy to slide down the slippery slope of self-bashing, I know what I'm talking about here because I've felt this way so many times after what I thought was the worst meeting/phone call/presentation I've ever had. If your head spins with "I was meant to do this or do that" situations, you're not in a position to make reasonable decisions about your results in this state of mind.

Your best bet is to take a step away from the situation, both physically and mentally, in order to gain an objective perspective. Taking a walk outside is a great way to relax your mind. Take a deep breath and keep reminding yourself of how great you are. It's important to come to a level-headed, emotionally neutral table to kick your drive into high gear.

Be grateful for what you've always achieved in life

EVERYONE IS ADVANCING in different stages than each other because basically everyone has a different view of what success is. You must be grateful for what you're doing right now, and for what you've done in life, rather than what you haven't. The only one who has such high expectations is YOU, so just trust that you're going to get there and don't set such a strict timetable on yourself. Setting your own goals is important, not just representing the expectations of others. Progress is a slow and steady journey, and one of the best ways to get there is through positivity and self-awareness. Make a list of minor accomplishments that you're particularly proud of. It can be small but important milestones that you'd like to brag about. Read it out loud to yourself every time you feel that self-criticism comes knocking at your door.

Treat yourself the way you would view a close friend

A GOOD WAY TO overcome negative self-criticism is to treat yourself as a friend. Would you choose any characteristic of their character to make them feel bad for themselves? The answer is probably no, so you need to treat yourself exactly the same way. You're your own best friend or your worst enemy, so take the time to be there both physically and emotionally. Encourage, listen, and remind yourself that everything is going to be right.

Change your "ego ideal" and remember: you are only human According to Freud's Psychoanalytical Theory of Psychology, the superego is a psychological aspect of the internalized values that we have inherited from our parents and society.

The ideal ego is a part of the superego and is often thought of like the picture we have of the ideal self of the person we want to become. It is this image that we hold as the ideal individual, often modeled after people we know, that we hold as the standard of who we are striving to be. As much as we would all love to be perfect, it's just not realistic. In fact, seeking an impossibly high standard will only lead to disappointment and self-criticism. Go easy on your own and change your priorities where appropriate. Maybe you're not fine, but who is?

After all, I am only human.

Identify the tone inside

WHAT'S YOUR THINKING? What do you expect from your inner critic? What is the best and worst scenario? Were you scared of something going on? You will start asking questions until you find your internal critical voice. Be curious about why these emotions are felt. This is a daunting method in which you know how to locate the source of the feeling. Take a step back to look at your inner critic as if someone were asking you these things instead of yourself. Use your smart mind to defend them.

Separate from the criticism inside

THE NEXT MOVE is to write down and record your thoughts on your mobile as well. The specifics should include all that happened at the time. Before the critic struck, what did you do? What were you doing until your mind was taken over by negative thoughts? What were the exact words that were said to be self-critical? You can take a step back when you do this and see the feelings in another way or from another viewpoint.

Answer the own criticism

YOU CAN THEN HAVE A MORE realistic assessment of yourself after writing down your thoughts and capturing your circumstance or environment. If your inner critic says, for example, "I can't get anything right. I'm not going to achieve my goals, "respond with," It's normal to make mistakes, and as a person, I'm going to fight, but I'm smart enough to know that I can achieve my goals if I choose. "This technique will reframe your brain to help you start looking at things differently so that your automatic response to disappointment will be a more rational solution over time. It shows love and worthiness for yourself.

Do not rely on your own critique

YOU KNOW what you're looking for. You are familiar with your principles. You know what you are capable of. That's why it would hurt your reputation to settle for anything less. Your inner critic should never have a say in how you are behaving or what you think is for sure one thing the inner critic is just in your head. You may choose to let negative thoughts govern you when you think about this way, or you may choose to fulfill your own destiny. Treat your inner critic as a poor friend, not helping you and not wanting the best of you. Recognize the negative thoughts, but don't tap into them.

It will become softer and more distant when you obey these four steps of defeating the inner critic, and you will become stronger. You will have the freedom to pursue your dreams if you take the necessary steps to liberate yourself from your internal judgment, and you will become more caring and considerate of yourself. When the inner critic is just a distant memory, that's when you can actually get out of the grip it took, and you can become a more positive person you deserve to be.

WHAT CONFIDENCE IS
ALL ABOUT

What confidence is all about

SOMETHING ABOUT CONFIDENCE is that building and growing takes a lot of time, but only seconds to collapse. True faith never really crumbles, however. Trust can start in infancy, or it can develop over time and become part of adulthood. Confidence is a particular feeling that people carry around with them, has been scientifically proven. Science has proven that they have high self-esteem and self-respect when someone is positive. You are strong leaders and are able to bounce back while dropping or passing through difficult times. Individuals who are unconfident, frequently underestimate themselves and focus on their weaknesses; thus, they cannot make a positive move or a leap forward. Our expectations are too high on their own, and when they fail, they continue to bash themselves. Trust is not about the mistakes you made. It's not even about people's other shortcomings. Trust is about realizing you are good enough and thinking you are good enough. It's about doing what you want and what you're most excited about without worrying you're going to fail or mess up.

Those who are positive realize they are not flawless, but embrace what they can do and let go of what they can't.

A lot of people, when a guy scores a lot of goals, say,' He's a great player,' because a goal is very valuable, but a great player is a player who can do everything in the game. He will support, inspire his teammates, give them confidence to move forward. It's someone who, when a group doesn't do well, becomes like a manager.

Here are a few characteristics established or learned by a confident person:

They've got poise

WALKING IN CONFIDENCE.

The main eye contact

ALWAYS LOOK at the person they're referring to because they're not afraid to look at someone in the eye.

.

87

Despite their ways, they are
powerful

WE HAVE guidelines that uphold their beliefs and are
careful about them. We remain true to themselves and
follow their own personal beliefs in life.

They're not sure of their presence

CONFIDENT PEOPLE DON'T CARE what others say about them because they think they look good, and they take pride in their appearance.

89

They are self-assured

THEY HAVE a great head on their shoulders and, because they are self-assured, they are willing to tackle almost anything.

They're doing the right thing

EVEN IF IT can harm oneself or somebody else, by doing the right thing, a confident person still feels better. We don't give in to peer pressure, and we know what they think is wrong in their bones. People have strong intuitions that are positive.

91

They're not terrified of being
right

WE ADMIT their mistakes when they're right, and they're thinking about them. I know when to apologize and when to press for what they need to be assertive.

They don't steal the spotlight

TRUSTING people aren't greedy because they don't need other people's attention to make them feel good. We know they are good enough for themselves and keep their own thoughts and feelings close to them. So they let the spotlight be on someone else.

93

They're not scared of being
ashamed

CONFIDENT PEOPLE ARE GOING to do stupid things at
random because they are not scared of being funny.

94

They're not talking down other
people

IN REALITY, because they know right from wrong, they are building up men. Confident people don't like spending their time on unnecessary drama and confrontation because they know it is bringing down their own values and self-respect.

They're self-assured

ANY PERSON who is comfortable will not accept excuses or lied to. You know when and when to make someone go home. Generally speaking, someone who needs to be supported and knows the difference will benefit the optimistic person.

While some people may find it easy to be optimistic, it may feel like a daunting task for others that is hard to succeed. Not all of these characteristics must be acquired by a confident person, but even possessing one or two of them is a good step in trust. Don't think about being comfortable. Feeling optimistic is not being selfish or self-centered. If you're true to yourself and you understand the big difference between honesty and narcissism, you're going to be fine and you're well on the way to being what you want to be.

Do You Think Confidence Comes Naturally Or Is It Learned?

CONFIDENCE SEEMS to come naturally to some men.

For others, it's something that needs to be worked on and developed.

Was confidence an inherent trait? We all have a friend or a coworker who exudes trust. There's nothing about their feathers. Criticism seems to slide right off their backs. We have no fear of taking risks, of trying new things, and even when they do not excel, they never hesitate to try again.

Yet, contrary to popular belief, faith is not a matter of genetic programming. You can change how you feel about yourself and your ability to succeed.

Confidence can be learned

IT CAN BE CULTIVATED, cultivated and developed. And there's really no limit to how confident you can learn to be.

You could never know what you're made of, because as you get into it, your ability helps you to go even further.

Indispensable Tips For Building More Self-Confidence

WHAT IS CONFIDENCE FOR YOU?

An important first step in building your faith is to discover your own unique brand of trust.

What's the confidence in you? What does that look like? How does it feel like that? Do you feel confident when you put on a hat, a coat, or a pair of shoes? Will you feel confident when you're in the center of a particular activity?

Which makes you feel good for yourself, huh? Consider the moments in your day and life that stand out for you as high points — the places where you feel relaxed, comfortable, and completely in charge.

Identify and challenge negative scripts

IT'S important to know what makes you feel good. But it is just as important to know what doesn't make you feel good.

Each of us has a pessimistic commentator in our heads the nagging little voice that criticizes us. If we trip, break, and make a mistake, there's a voice that makes a mean, feeling-bad comment. They're running misleading scripts that kill our self-esteem.

We can really be our own worst enemy. Learn to identify and challenge negative scripts in your mind. Is what you just told yourself to be true? It's certainly not.

Self Esteem And Self Confidence

SELF-ESTEEM AND SELF-CONFIDENCE have many simi-larities and differences, as well. Both are called how you feel about yourself; but, generally, self-esteem is more about how you feel about yourself. Self-esteem is how much self-love and good feelings you have for yourself, while self-confidence focuses primarily on your skills. Someone may have high self-esteem, but in certain aspects of their lives they may not be very comfortable, such as how they are in subjects like math. You develop self-esteem by learning how to take care of yourself, building your self-worth, identifying who you are, and respecting yourself through your flaws. High self-esteem comes from knowing that you deserve to be cared for, that you are worthy, and that you value your-self. So as you increase your total sense of value, you also raise your level of confidence.

Creating self-confidence, in other words, comes from your outward encounters, while self-esteem comes from an internal experience. Self-esteem refers to how from within we think about ourselves. This represents our relationship with our own sense of entitlement. Self-confidence represents how, as we go through different circumstances and paths, we see ourselves in the outside world.

YOU MUST DO the following to build and improve your self-esteem:

- Talk to your (intuition) true self.
- Challenge the criticism inside.
- Be good to yourself.
- Take care of yourself and do what you want to do.
- Also, recompense yourself.
- Help others and be careful with your process of learning.
- Validate the accomplishments you have made.

SOMEONE CAN TRUST MORE than they have self-esteem or more self-esteem than they value. Having said that, if we have more self-esteem and less faith, if we lose, we will end up being more robust. This is because our self-image falls before our higher level of confidence, so when we mess up, it serves as a cornerstone. If we have a lower level of confidence but less self-esteem, due to the constant pessimistic noise inside our minds, we may not feel very good about our achievements. As you can see, it's probably more detrimental to have low self-esteem than confidence. When you focus on your self-esteem, though, you will also strive to improve your level of confidence. You can support yourself by doing the things listed above to achieve a higher level of self-esteem in which trust can come to you instinctively and immediately.

How Negative Thoughts Affect Our Life And Actions

AS YOU SLEEP, your subconscious mind takes over, and when you wake up, your subconscious mind's thoughts come into your conscious mind. Some of these thoughts are "Wake up," "No, I'm asleep," "I'm too sleepy," "Time to take a bath," "I'm so lazy," "The dream was funny." Also, uncontrollable are the unconscious feelings that we have, so they come up at random moments. But in fact, we are in charge of what is happening to our subconscious minds. The more we feel one way, the more our mind gets stuck. And if we choose to think positively, we'll wake up over time and think positively. If we permit our inner opponents to take control, then most negative thoughts flow through. The product of our subconscious minds is our actions. Our actions are based on the minds moving into our brains. When you learn how to control your subconscious mind, you can actually help make your life feel better and more optimistic. When you feel better, you will also feel more confident.

Three things you can do to reprogram your subconscious mind is to use positive self-talk, pledge to change your negative thoughts, and pursue a more compassionate (rational) way of thinking. Watch them if you know that your emotions are pessimistic or gloomy. Substitute them with a positive statement after that. For more guidance on how to let go of the unconscious critic, see section 2. It's so important to reprogram your subconscious mind because if you let it take over, it's going to ruin your life. All that comes into your brain must serve as part of your actions. Simply put, you're putting negative energy into the world when you think negatively, and bad things are going to happen. You will give positive energies to the world if you encourage positivity, and good things will happen to you. The way you see it is all about your thinking and your understanding of it. Basically, it's up to you to choose, so it's smart to sit down and list all the things you want to get in your life. What kind of person would you like to be? Where will you end up? What's the most important thing right now for you? Such questions will help you stay on track when it comes to positive thinking and having a sense of trust.

Recently, a survey of more than 30,000 people found that harping on negative life experiences (especially through rumination and self-denial) could be the primary indicator of some of today's most prevalent mental health problems. U.K. eye-opening performance. Research, the biggest of its kind, has shown that it is not just what happens to us that matters, but how we feel about it that forms our emotional well-being.

"While we understand that a person's genes and life conditions related to mental health problems, the results of this study have shown that traumatic life experiences are the main reason people suffer from anxiety and depression. Furthermore, the way a person feels about and interacts with stressful events is just as much a predictor of the level of stress and anxiety they experience," said lead researcher Peter Ki.

While self-reflection may be a key ingredient in a healthy, positive life, these new findings seem to drive home the point that rumination is just not good for us. Therefore, while I urge people to pursue self-understanding as a way of resolving personal struggles and becoming their truest selves, I strongly believe that this must be achieved with self-compassion. In order to face any obstacle without engaging in self-hatred and self-doubt, each and every one of us should follow what my mentor, psychologist and mindfulness specialist Dr. Daniel Siegel called a COAL attitude, in which they are Curious, Open, Accepting and Loving toward themselves.

Armed with this mindset, people are best able to fight one of the toughest challenges they will encounter in life: their own internal critic. "Critical inner voice" is a term that I often bring to new audiences. It is the foundation of a philosophy and counseling methodology founded by my father's psychiatrist and researcher, Dr. Robert Firestone. It is the basis of the book that we co-authored, Conquer Your Vital Inner Voice, and the topic of many of my lectures and webinars. Why I have invested so much of my time and work on this topic is that what I have found in my 30 years of research and clinical practice is that, in almost all situations, we are our own worst enemy.

This enemy's word is the vital inner voice. It is an unconscious conversation that contributes to rumination, self-denial, and self-denial. It mocks us, it shames us, it threatens us, and it lures us into self-limiting and self-destructive behavior. This asks us not to trust the people we love. This affects us not to try to reach a target. This guides us and subdues us, keeping us seemingly secure inside a miserable, but familiar, body.

Each one of us has this voice in one form or another. Yours may be more focused on your work. "Don't go after that promotion; just accept where you are. You're not capable of success." Maybe it's going to teach you about your love life. "Don't keep dating. It's pointless. No one will ever love you. You're destined to be alone." Maybe, like most of us, there's an optimistic, self-compassionate and ambitious side of you, but you're also divided. And while one hand is goal-directed so life-asserting, the other is self-critical, self-hating, and ultimately self-destructive.

As a result, the most important battle you can face is the one that's going on inside you, the actual one that's going on against your vital inner voice. The good news is that this is a battle you should win. As Kinderman said in his study, "While we can't change a person's family history or life experience, it's possible to help a person change their way of thinking and teach them positive coping strategies that can mitigate and reduce stress."

You may start this process by following a zero-tolerance policy for your "voices" and self-destructive behavior. Because these beliefs have been deeply entrenched since childhood, it may be difficult to distinguish your negative inner voices from your actual observations and sense of self. The "sound" can be elusive and have an effect on your attitude in ways that seem slight. It could draw on things that are real. Of starters, if you're a shy person, it might warn you, "You're so self-conscious; don't go to that party. Just stay home and read. You're just going to feel awkward and out of place." Very often, we listen to these feelings without really being mindful that we're getting them.

As a result, the first step in battling your inner critic is to know when he speaks up. When are you going to strike yourself? What kind of causes, big or small, set it off? Is it taking part in a social event? Are you talking at a meeting, huh? Are you asking someone out of here? When you begin to notice the situations that cause sounds, you can recognize trends in your emotions and become more mindful of them. In reality, you can know when you strike yourself. In addition, you will be better equipped to resist listening to these thoughts.

The next move may sound the easiest, but it may be the most difficult. As soon as you note that a sound begins to resonate in your head, stop it! Stop the way of thinking without question. Have zero tolerance of anything you're told by this inner enemy. Another technique for overcoming obsessive-compulsive disorder is to convince yourself that your mind is lying to you. Once you start to think properly, you should note, "It's not me; it's my OCD." The same goes for your inner critic. "This isn't me. This is my vital inner voice. Such feelings are not my guilt trying to keep me on track; they are an internal foe trying to take me off course and keep me away from my interests and goals.

An example that a lot of people can relate to is trying on clothes. You start cataloging tiny defects in your face, looking in the mirror. You've got feelings like "my legs are too scrawny" and "ouch, I hate my thighs." Soon, the thoughts are escalating. "You're too gross. You're not doing hard. You're not going to look beautiful. You're hideous!" You went from being in a good mood, getting dressed in the morning, and shopping with a friend, to feeling depressed or demoralized. As a result, you show less confidence throughout the day.

That's why you need to enforce a zero-tolerance policy at the first hint that your inner critic is at the wheel. Don't encourage yourself to worry about what they're doing. There's nothing to do with it, no statement to consider, no point of view to entertain. It's just rumination in action. Be wary of thoughts that sound kind or seductive. "It's all right that you're alone. You're all right on your own; you don't need anybody."

Be careful with voices that sound paradoxical or self-aggrandizing to others. "No one sees your potential.

They don't appreciate you. They're just jealous of you." While these thought processes may sound sympathetic or even complimentary, they leave you empty and often head in the opposite direction to your goals. Plus, when you operate on these emotions, there are more important self-attacks waiting to welcome you. "You're there again, all alone. What a loser!"

If you find yourself overthinking, or you realize that your emotions have turned negative, you're much better off avoiding the rumination and taking action against them instead. Part of zero tolerance is not allowing these voices to influence your actions. If you're told to be alone, invite a friend to have some tea. If your career achievement is compensated, apply for that senior position. Take actions that will take you back to your most authentic self. You can expect your voices to get louder when you first change something about yourself. But the more you persevere in your deeds, the quieter they will become. It's hard to attack yourself for being lazy when you exercise regularly or when you actively pursue your goals.

A new longitudinal review of studies has shown that mindfulness-based and cognitive-behavioral interventions can be effective in reducing both rumination and anxiety. They say, "More generally, it suggests that interventions that allow patients to change their thought style or to disengage from emotional response to rumination and/or anxiety could be beneficial."

In addition, Dr. Kristin Neff's research has shown that, compared to self-esteem, self-compassion is associated with greater emotional resilience, more accurate self-concepts, more caring relationship behavior, and less narcissism and reactive anger. Like self-esteem, self-compassion is not based on appraisal, but on a fundamental sense of human dignity. Dr. Neff describes self-compassion as a kind, linked, and clear-sighted way of relating to ourselves even in situations of loss, perceived inadequacy, and imperfection.

In introducing zero tolerance, we are evicting what Arianna Huffington refers to as the "unholy tenant" in our minds. The way to do this is by being mindful of and not listening to these emotions, practicing self-compassion and working against the instructions of your inner critic, not allowing this internal foe to control your life.

HOW TO SURMOUNT YOUR EMOTIONS AND ACCEPT YOURSELF

How to surmount your emotions and accept yourself

MARK TWAIN ONCE SAID, "The worst isolation is not to be happy with yourself." When you finally accept yourself and your weaknesses, your life is going to be much more freeing.

According to Dr. Tara Brach, founder of Radical Self-Acceptance, thoughts of guilt and indignity are the root of many issues that we face in our friendships, professions and artistic activities.

Self-acceptance is the ability to accept yourself as you are, instead of the way you wish you were, or the way you expect others to view you. This frees you from being too concerned about what other people are saying about you.

Self-acceptance is a feeling of satisfaction with yourself despite your weaknesses and regardless of your past behaviors and choices. This is necessary for good mental health.

Once we recognize ourselves, we will welcome all aspects of ourselves not just the good parts. Self-acceptance could be the secret to a happier life, but it is the positive habit that many people practice the least.

As Robert Holden put it in his book, Happiness now! "Happiness and self-acceptance are going hand in hand. Actually, your level of self-acceptance determines your level of happiness. The more self-acceptance you get, the more pleasure you will be able to accept, gain and appreciate. In other words, you deserve as much satisfaction as you think you are capable of[emphasis added]. You can accept it and still work on being the best version of yourself.

Nass, a professor of communications at Stanford University, explains, "Negative emotions generally require more thinking, and data is analyzed more deeply than positive."

Typical human action relies on negative qualities. People who judge themselves negatively handle negative emotions rather than negative ones. Which means they spend more time considering bad things, and less time on good things.

They are much better consumers of our vulnerabilities than our advantages, "said Ryan Howes, Ph.D., a psychologist in Pasadena, California.

This can quickly become a loop that is difficult to break.

Going through life happily allows us to consider the combination of positive and negative feelings and to strive to embrace ourselves and becoming the best versions of ourselves.

Self-acceptance starts with purpose, "said psychotherapist Jeffrey Sumber, MA. "It is important that we give ourselves the expectation that we are willing to shift paradigms from the world of guilt, suspicion and humiliation to the world of equality, empathy, recognition and confidence," he said.

Self-loathing and poor self-acceptance does not

contribute to a satisfying life. Living of self-acceptance is much better than a life of self-hatred.

You can even go a leap further by writing down your skills. That puts things in perspective for you. Start with something basic like "I'm a kind person." If you're having trouble coming up with things you're great about, ask your friends and colleagues to help. Sometimes, people close to us are best off knowing our greatest strengths. Don't pressure everything to be published in a single sitting. Usually, the lists are changing over time.

Howes recommends that you make a different kind of list to raise your faith and understand how far you've come. He adds, "Make a list of all the challenges you've faced, all the dreams you've accomplished, all the friendships you've created, and all the lives you've changed for the good. Keep it close, update it regularly, and often add to it.

With enough preparation and a change of outlook on yourself, you can stop judging yourself and stop harming yourself with the severe impact of negative self-judgment.

It will take time for the path to self-acceptance. Our external circumstances, past experiences, and how we were brought up can make it difficult for us to embrace ourselves. But this isn't difficult. Over time, you will slowly grow into a state of complete self-acceptance. Sometimes it helps to seek the help of our loved ones or the specialist if things get too tough.

One of the greatest gifts that you can offer yourself is self-acceptance.

In the words of the psychiatrist Tara Brach: "Imperfection is not our personal problem, it is a natural part of our existence. The limit of what we can consider is the frontier of our rights.

Self-acceptance is the key feature of self-love and self-esteem building. It's when on a deeper level you know and understand yourself, but you're all right with all you are. You are acknowledging your shortcomings, and you know what is good for you. Self-acceptance is about realizing that during the cycle of personal growth, you will develop on the basis of these strengths and weaknesses and be fully compassionate with yourself. When you look at yourself every day and feel as if you are disappointed and dissatisfied with yourself, the path to approval of yourself is to tell yourself why. Would you like someone else to be you? What's that you don't like so much about yourself? Is it the presence of you? Is it the character of you? The good thing is that it is possible to change or adjust identities, and so impressions can be. This will have a more dramatic effect. You will start improving your life by learning how to understand your patterns and actions and stop comparing yourself to other people. The most important step in learning how to embrace yourself is to strive for self-growth. Another can't really understand who they are unless they really know who they are.

This is what self-acceptance feels like:

- Loving yourself for who you are
- Trust your personality, talents, and presentation
- Be caring about yourself
- Not being judgmental about yourself and your shortcomings
- Being able to admit and accept your shortcomings
- Knowing that your background doesn't affect you, so you don't have to focus on it

YOU CAN LEARN to live with them and learn from them when you see your errors. The only thing you can control is to accept your present position as it is right now, so it's your responsibility to make the most of this moment. You will find ways to improve in areas of your life that you are not so proud of by seeing your mistakes and learning to live completely at the moment. This might be your career; you might not be doing what you love. Part of accepting yourself is acknowledging that you don't like what you're doing but at the same time seeking ways to do later what you love. For example, if you're working as a professional cleaner, but you're passionate about being a mechanic, you're brainstorming ideas on how to save money to get to the first step of doing this. Ask yourself what stands in your dream's way. Fight and go for those barriers. You can decrease the feelings of anger and resentment toward yourself when you learn self-improvement strategies and actually do what you wanted to do. The first step in doing what you love is to change your negative state of mind, being who you want to be and branching out to better things.

There are many techniques that promote personal growth and acceptance of oneself. Here are a few of them:

- Observing your thoughts and actions consciously
- Modifying your way of thinking (that is, questioning the inner critic)
- Repeating optimistic mantras in stressful times

MANY PEOPLE DON'T FIND it easy to accept themselves. That's why so many people are reading books for self-help and taking classes for depression. Life is much easier when we are children, or at least it should be. Then we become adults from our youth. We want our wings to be stretched and defiant. We are really trying to define who we are in this process. We turn ourselves into the kind of adults we want to be. Once we're teenagers, most of us don't understand what we're doing. Adulthood is arriving too soon. In this life, the things we are passing through shape us and our minds. That's why respecting ourselves and embracing who we really are right now may be too hard for some of us. Many events mess with our confidence in the adolescent years. There's very heavy peer pressure. As adults, we feel like we're going to have to blend in or look in and act a way to get admitted. As children, our parents may not have shown the love and support we wanted. Many people may have chronic problems with alienation and substance abuse. Many children in foster families may have had to grow up, so they already feel unloved and unwanted in the community. We're turning our impressions into who we are now. Self-acceptance means recognizing what influenced you, but not having the background to determine who you want to be. It's about changing your mind and challenging the misconceptions of what you've been told by people, knowing it's never too late to evolve into what you deserve.

Ask yourself, "Who do I want to be?" Is it a confident businessman/woman? Is it a nurturing parent? Is it a creative loner? Then ask yourself, "Who am I now?" Is it a reserved friend? A selfish spouse? A broken individual? Finally, say this to yourself, "It doesn't matter who I am today, what got me here, and who I am going to become. What matters is that I am here, I am who I am, and I am proud." In reality, this is all that self-acceptance truly is just knowing what you want, being able to define who you are, and not allowing the past to shape you. If you have the ability to wipe the slate clean and start over or if you (God forbid) get in a horrible accident that wipes your memories and you have the chance to restart your life, what would you do with it? Whatever the answer is, start from there. Keeping that in mind, here are a few tips on how to start your road to self-acceptance:

BE GOOD TO YOURSELF!

- The first step in accepting yourself is that you need to let go of being so critical and judgmental of yourself. The only person who criticizes you more than anyone else is you, so practice kindness. You can practice kindness by doing the following
- Reward yourself for big and small achievements.
- Treat yourself once a month or once every two weeks.
- Save 10 percent of your paycheck.
- Relax more.
- Become best friends with yourself and learn more about yourself.
- Implement some "me time" every day.
- Don't take on too much for you to handle.

Confront your worries

IT MIGHT BE your inner critic who makes you scared, or the mistakes that hold you back. You might have a pattern of overthinking, or you might be someone who needs to control certain situations. Facing your worries head-on, instead of getting stuck, you can keep moving on. It's easy to do what you do, and it's frightening and unpredictable to do something different. If you want to see progress, though, you need to take baby steps towards it. Having a list of things that you dread with your goals is a good starting point.

Here are a few things you can do to confront your worries:

- Make a list of your anxieties and goals.
- Build a ladder of terror (explained in chapter 6).
- To help you conquer your anxiety, write motivational quotations.
- Every day, change one thing.
- Sit for a little while with your anxiety, then slowly expand it.

Practice positive performance

PRACTICING positivity will help you keep track of your ambitions. In this situation, your goal is to make yourself more valued and embraced. Observe the feeling and substitute it with a positive affirmation if your inner critic sneaks on you. When you look at your world and your group of friends, decide what can be modified, what can be improved, and what is the most beneficial for you.

Here are a few positive things you can do:

- Always have a good quotation folder on you.
- Have sticky notes around your house, so every day you can say something positive about yourself.
- For a positive lift, call a helpful and optimistic person.
- Do something that's interesting.
- Begin a new hobby.

No one is flawless

YOU'RE NOT PERFECT, so why aspire to be ideal? Each fault you have, such as your frizzy hair, your freckles, your character instability, all compensates for who you are. Self-acceptance doesn't mean what your experience describes you to be; it's more about being able to look at yourself in the mirror and accept all the imperfections in you. So you've been fucking up at work and turning red in your white clothes. You may say something out of spite or respond to your emotions impulsively. Know these things happen, and all you can do is leave it there while it's in the past. The effort to change. If you can rectify a relationship and make an error, do so. When you can't, learn to accept that you are who you are incomplete.

There's nothing wrong with it. Here are some stuff that will help you put imperfections into practice:

- Don't stick to the background.
- Be patient on your own.
- Don't think about confrontation.

- Change what you can change, and let yourself sort out everything else.
- Remember your mistakes and make funny a tough situation.
- Look crazy and dumb.
- Intentionally dance and sing badly.

Believe in yourself

MANY PEOPLE ARE STRUGGLING because they feel insecure if they can do something or not. You are simply
setting yourself up for failure by getting this frame of
mind. For example, if you're planning for a speech and
you're thinking, "I can't do that," "I'm going to collapse
totally," "What if everybody likes it?" You're going to
deliver your speech thinking you're going to screw it up,
make you nervous, and eventually screw it up. On the
other hand, if you go into it saying, "I'm nervous, but
I've got it all," "I'm going to nail it," "If I'm not doing
well, it's not going to be as bad as I'm making it seem,"
you're setting yourself up to conquer your fear of
speech, and you're building self-confidence that boosts
your self-esteem overall. Believe in your own name. You
can do whatever you want to do. You've been worse
through or lived since. Think of all the times that you
got up after a mistake and when it threatened to get you
down, it rocked life.

Here are some things that you can do to exercise
your self-belief:

- Move the anxiety and misconceptions and prejudices past.
- Don't worry about what other people say.
- Stay up for it.
- Create as many mantras as you can. "Can't" is literally a "can" term with a T.
- Confide in yourself. Trust that every encounter is an opportunity to grow regardless of the outcome.
- Push past the discomfort or fears and myths.
- Put yourself out there, not caring what other people think.
- Stay positive.
- Create mantras that you can. "Can't" is just the word "can" with a T.
- Trust yourself. Trust that no matter the outcome, every experience is an opportunity to grow.

If we struggle

WE'RE LEARNING what we can do and what we can do differently. We only get to understand ourselves on a deeper level by our errors, so push past the fear of rejection, forget the inner critic, trust that you will excel, and stand up if you fall down. Find your motivation, find out what inspires you most, target your goals, and try to be better at what you're not good at. It can motivate you to do these things more easily and over time. You will continue to see that things don't always end badly, and you will also increase your self-esteem.

HERE ARE some more robust things you can do:

- Be self-supporting.
- Be definitive and strong.
- Building efficient barriers.
- Know that it is part of life to change.
- Check for opportunities for self-discovery.
- Do what's right for you, and change what you're not.

If you don't recognize yourself

YOUR ATTITUDE MUST BE MODIFIED. As difficult as this can be, the most important thing you can do when it comes to personal development is perhaps improving your attitude. You will continue to find things you learn best as you develop an understanding of yourself. What is it that makes you feel good? What's going to help you reach for it? Is there anybody who can help you? For your own personal understanding of what it is all about to embrace who you are, these are crucial questions to answer. It takes time to do anything and everything you do (whether developing a new hobby or learning a new skill). When you're committed to respecting who you are, you're showing your brain how to control yourself, which will set your mind to do other things like positive thinking, feeling optimistic, and taking care of yourself.

A competency is something that you need to know.

LEARN TO STAY FOCUSED AND BE COMPASSIONATE WITH YOURSELF BY TAKING THE FOLLOWING STEPS

Acknowledging How You Think
About Yourself

A SELF-CONCEPT IS an understanding you have of yourself that's based on your personal experiences, body image, your thoughts, and how you tend to label yourself in various situations.

A self-concept can also be defined as an all-encompassing awareness you had of yourself in the past; the awareness you have of yourself in the present, and the expectations you have of yourself at a future time.

Your self-concept is built upon perception — upon how you perceive yourself based on the knowledge you have gained over a lifetime of experience.

When it comes down to it, a self-concept is a perception you have of your image, abilities, and in some ways a perception of your own individual uniqueness.

This perception you have of yourself is based on the information you have gathered about your values, life roles, goals, skills, and abilities over time.

Your self-concept is somewhat a collection of beliefs you have about your own nature, qualities, and behavior. It's about how you think and evaluate yourself at any given moment in time.

But to truly understand what a self-concept is and its impact on your life, we first need to break down the three components of a self-concept. These three components are based on the work of Humanist Psychologist Carl Rogers.

Your Self Image

YOUR SELF-IMAGE COMES DOWN to how you see yourself in the present moment. This includes the labels you give yourself about your personality and the beliefs you have about how the external world perceives you.

It's, however, important to note that your self-image isn't necessarily based on reality. For instance, a person with anorexia may have a self-image that makes them believe they are obese, however, in reality, that is far from the truth.

Given this, it's crucial to recognize that a self-image is only your own perception of yourself and has no real basis in reality.

109

Your Self-Ideal

YOUR SELF-IDEAL IS how you wish you could be at a future time. This is your ideal self or the ideal person you envision of being and becoming.

Many times, how people see themselves and how they would like to see themselves doesn't quite match up. And this is precisely what causes problems and often leads to self-sabotaging behavior patterns and emotional struggles.

Your Self-Esteem

YOUR SELF-ESTEEM ENCOMPASSES your current emotional experiences. Moreover, it refers to the extent to which you like or approve of yourself or the extent to which you value yourself.

You might, for instance, have a positive or negative view of yourself. When you have a negative picture of yourself, you are seen as having low self-esteem. This often manifests in a lack of confidence and pessimism.

On the other hand, when you have a favorable view of yourself you are seen as having high self-esteem. This often manifests in a confident disposition, self-acceptance, and optimism.

Acknowledge your strengths and attributes

RECOGNIZING YOUR STRENGTHS, or attributes that you value, to help balance the work you do on accepting parts of yourself that are less valued. In fact, knowing your strengths will help you change your outlook about yourself. Start by naming your strengths, and list one strength per day if it's hard to think about them.
For starters:

- I am a loving person.
- I'm a powerful mother.
- I'm a professional artist.
- I'm a creative problem solver.

Make a list of your accomplishments

IDENTIFY and acknowledge your strengths by listing your achievements. These may include individuals you've helped, your personal accomplishments, and difficult times you've overcome. Those sorts of reminders may help you focus on acts and behavior. Further concrete examples can allow you to recognize your abilities.

For instance:

- My father's death was a painful one for our parents, but I am grateful that I have been able to help support my mom through suffering.
- I set out to run a half-marathon, and after six months of training, I crossed the finish line!
- After losing my job, it was hard to adjust to pay bills, but I've learned a lot about my own power, and now I'm in a better place.

Recognize how you judge yourself

RECOGNIZING your own judgment is important in helping you to identify areas where you are overly critical of yourself. Getting overly critical is that when you build places and consider qualities of yourself, you have unproductive emotions about it. These may involve guilt and frustration, and these emotions may kill self-acceptance. Start writing a list of negative thoughts you might have about yourself.

For instance:

- I'm not going to be able to do anything wrong.
- I still take the comments of others the wrong way; something has to be wrong with me.
- Okay, I'm too fat.
- I'm terrible at decision making.

114

Recognize how other people's comments affect you

WHEN OTHER PEOPLE make comments about us, we often internalize these comments and work on our own opinions. If you can work out the origin of your own assumptions, you can help to reconsider how you view yourself. For instance:

If your mom has always questioned your appearance, you may not be very positive about your looks right now. But understand that her criticism was rooted in her own insecurities. When you know this, you will start to reconsider your faith in your looks.

CHALLENGING YOUR
INNER CRITIC

Catch yourself when you think negative thoughts

WHEN YOU KNOW the different areas of your life that you are most dismissive of, it's time to begin to silence your "inner critic." Your inner critic tells you things like, "I'm not the ideal body type" or "I can never do anything wrong." Quiet your inner critic will minimize the impact of your negative thoughts about yourself that will help you create space for empathy, forgiveness, and forgiveness. To silence the inner critic, practice catching up with these negative thoughts when they come up.

For example, when you find yourself saying, "I'm such an idiot," ask yourself these things:

- Is that a generous feeling for you?
- Does that make me feel good?
- Is that what I'd say to a friend or loved one?
- If these answers are no, then you know that your internal critic is speaking again.

Challenge your inner critic

IF YOU FIND yourself thinking negative thoughts about yourself, threaten and silence this inner critic. Always ready with a constructive counter-think and slogan. You can use the advantages you've learned in previous steps. For instance:

- When you find yourself thinking, "I'm unintelligent," change your mind to a kind statement: "Though I may not understand this topic, I'm smart in other respects, and that's good."
- Consider your strengths: "We're not all skilled in the same stuff. I know that my talent and skill are in another field, and I am proud of that. "
- Consider your inner critic that the derogatory statement is not true. "Alright, internal critic, I know you're used to thinking that I'm not intelligent, but that's not real. I learn that I have the strength of intelligence in important and specific ways.

- Make sure always to be kind to your own critic. Remember to educate yourself, because you're still trying to change your feelings about yourself.

Focus on self-acceptance first before self-improvement

Self-acceptance is just accepting yourself as you are in the present. Self-improvement reflects on the improvements that need to be made in order to recognize yourself in the future. Identify areas intended to be valued as they are now. Then you can decide whether or not you want to develop them in the future.

You might want to lose weight, for instance. First start with a self-acceptance declaration about your current body weight: "Even though I want to lose weight, I'm great and I feel good just like I am." Instead, frame your self-improvement in optimistic, constructive terms. Instead of saying, "I'm not the ideal body type, and when I lose 20 pounds, I'm going to be healthy and feel good," you may suggest, "I'd like to lose 20 pounds to make me happier and more power."

Alter expectations of yourself

IF YOU SET your own unrealistic expectations, you set yourself up for failure. It, in effect, will make it hard to embrace yourself. Turn your standards for yourself.

For example, when you say, "I'm so lazy. I haven't swept the kitchen yet, "I change the standards and say," I've got dinner for the whole family. I can get the kids to help clean up the kitchen tomorrow after dinner.

CREATING COMPASSION
FOR YOURSELF

Learn that you are worthy of compassion

IT MAY SEEM strange and awkward to suggest that you have empathy for yourself, because it may seem self-centered, but self-compassion is the cornerstone for self-acceptance. This is because empathy is the "sympathetic knowledge of the suffering of others with a wish to ease it." You deserve the same consideration and love! The first step in self-compassion is to affirm your self-esteem. It is simple and quite popular to cause the emotions, perceptions, opinions and beliefs of others to determine our self-approval. Instead of making your agreement to be the judgment of others, make it your own. Learn to verify and support yourself without the need of others.

Practice daily affirmations

AN AFFIRMATION IS a positive statement that is meant to encourage and uplift. Using this method for yourself can be a powerful tool to help build self-compassion. Having compassion for yourself makes it easier for you to empathize and forgive your past self, which will help you overcome feelings of guilt and regret. Daily assertions also help to change the inner critic steadily. Develop sympathy on a daily basis by saying, reading, and thought words.

Types of statements include:

- I'm in a position to get through tough times; I'm smarter than I feel.
- I'm not flawless and I make mistakes, and that's all right.
- I'm a kind and compassionate mother of mine.
- Take a break from empathy. If you're having a tough day acknowledging a part of yourself, take a moment and be kind and develop your self-compassion. Recognize that your opinion of yourself causes pain and that self-judgment

can be overly harsh. Try to be kind and practice self-assertion.

FOR INSTANCE: when you think, "I'm not the ideal body shape; I'm overweight," admit that these feelings are unkind to yourself: "These are unkind thoughts, and I wouldn't say to a friend. They make me feel miserable and useless.

"Say something kind:" My body may not be flawless, but it's mine and it's safe, and it helps me to do things that I enjoy, including playing with my kids.

Practice forgiveness

PRACTICING self-forgiveness may help to reduce the sense of guilt of your experience, which may stop you from fully accepting your life. You can judge your history on the basis of unrealistic expectations. Forgive yourself will raise your guilt and giving you room to build a fresh, more positive view of your experience. Often our internal detractors are hesitant to let us forgive ourselves for the past.

Sometimes we are unkind to ourselves by bringing our remorse around us. Take special note of the shame that you may have. Try to assess what other factors are involved in the case. Events are sometimes out of our control, but we still hold on to those feelings of guilt. Evaluate whether the acts are completely out of your reach or ready to forgive in excess.

To help you achieve self-forgiveness, writing a letter can be a strong emotional and cognitive resource to start the process. Write a letter to your younger and former self, and use a sweet, caring voice. Consider your younger self (inner critic) that you may have made mistakes. Yet you know you're not fine, and that's all right. Our errors often provide valuable learning opportunities. Recall what you acted, or what you did, maybe it was something you know what to do at that time.

Turn guilt thoughts into gratitude statements

REMEMBERING that you often learn from past mistakes can help you think productively about your past. Practice being thankful for what you've learned, and accept that making mistakes is part of life. So your previous regret and embarrassment won't keep you from embracing yourself in the present. Write down the remorse phrases/thoughts that you have, and turn each of them into a grateful message. For instance:

Unkind thought/inner critic: I was mean to my parents when I was 20 years old. I'm so sorry I've been acting that way.

Message of Gratitude: I am thankful that I knew about actions at that age, because it was useful to raise my own children.

Unkind thought/inner critic: I ripped my life apart because I couldn't stop drinking.

Confirmation of Gratitude: I am thankful that I can rebuild friendships and try again in the future.

Getting Help

SURROUND yourself with people who love you. When you spend your time around people who deny your self-esteem, you may have a hard time accepting yourself. If people are continually dismissive of you, it's going to be harder to persuade yourself that you have advantages. Spend time with people who support you and love you. Such people are going to give you the support you need to embrace yourself for who you are.

See a therapist

A THERAPIST CAN HELP you peel back the barriers that might stop you from embracing yourself. This person can help you explore your past to understand why you're thinking a few things about yourself. He can also help you come up with ways to talk to yourself, make suggestions for self-assertion, and so on.

Establish boundaries and communicate assertively with others

ESTABLISH boundaries and interact with others. If you do need to communicate with people who are critical or who are not welcoming, you may need to set boundaries. Talk to these people so they can understand how unproductive and hurtful their words are.

For example, if your supervisor is always dismissive of your job, you can say, "I feel like I don't get enough support for my project. I want to do a good job, but I think it's hard to impress you. Let's hammer out a compromise that will work for both of us.

Changing Your State Of Mind

CHANGING your state of mind is not just recognizing the positive, but realizing what holds you back from your full potential. Acceptance of your flaws and strengthening your shortcomings are just a small part of learning what you can do about personal growth and self-esteem. The attitude is a big part that stops most of us from focusing on ourselves. Most of our problems are caused by a destructive or unhelpful state of mind. We are held back by negative thinking. The inner detractors are going to stop us from moving forward. Don't think too much about what it teaches us. One thing is certain if you feel miserable and lonely; the feeling grows in your head. You need a mentality that encourages your efforts if you want to be optimistic and effective. Often for affirmation, we look to others, and we don't get it. What you should do is look at yourself inwardly for the reassurance and affirmation you are looking for. It's time to get rid of the contagious depressive state of mind and enter a world where you're not second-guessing, stressing, overthinking, or vulnerable to vulnerability. Here is a list of negative thought habits that make you insecure and lack of self-love:

Scarcity

THIS IS the belief that you are not sufficient and that you are not sufficient. Cash, incentives, opportunities, manpower, etc. are not enough. The truth of the matter is that it will always be true what you think is true. So if you feel like there's not enough, then it won't be enough resources and things. Prepare your mind to think it's enough, and it's going to be.

Other

THIS IS the assumption that the root of all the issues is something or someone else. It's an illusion you're not right, but somewhere you point the blame. Their struggles, their tragedy, and their issues are never someone else's fault. You are always responsible for your choices. The result you will benefit from is determined by your choices. Thinking others are responsible for your misfortunes is thinking you lack the power to alter or choose. The reality is that nobody has the power to change your attitude or your mistakes; it is you and you alone who have this power.

Imposter

IMPOSTER SYNDROME IS CAUSED by a lack of confidence. This is the belief that other people may find that you don't seem to be who you are. That assumption is going to kill your hopes and rob you of the talents you still have to seek. Be who you want to be, and assume that you don't know you well enough to make that judgment by anyone who knows less than you do.

Cynicism

THIS WAY of thinking makes a person feel he can't trust anyone or put his faith in anyone. If you are suspicious of other people's intentions, so you encourage yourself to sit by and try to handle things on your own. Although freedom is a positive feature, it may be the one thing that stands in the way of your success not to put your faith in someone else.

Ungrateful

THE LACK of gratitude means you don't understand what you've got because you're always looking for more. You don't even have the gratitude for believing that what you have is good enough, even if you get more. Striving for more is okay; nevertheless, being appreciative of the stuff you now have is an attractive quality in anybody, and it shows great confidence.

Entitlement

THIS TYPE of belief revolves around thinking you have the right to have or obtain anything you want without suffering consequences or working for something. It's the thought life is going to hand you stuff because you're special and above all else. When you think this way, it's like waiting for someone to realize you deserve something in most cases, it never arrives. Feeling this way can create a sense of indignity and make you and others around you feel resentful. By doing something for others without wanting to be heard, undo this idea. Pay yourself for what you think is worthwhile rather than looking for someone else.

Nihilism

DOES your life have no meaning? Do you feel like you're spinning without intent or direction in circles? This is regarded as nihilism. It is the belief that your life does not have any meaning or purpose. Success is about the true love and intent being revealed. Everyone is good at something, but they're doing something else because they know it and they know it. Search and fight for something worth fighting for. So you're going to find true meaning.

Such ways of thinking are addictive and can take control of how you see the world and all that's in it. Pessimism is the source of these negative mindset habits, and it will reverse the effects these behaviors have on you by introducing positivity in your life. Be mindful of these forms of thought and attitudes and then replace them with positive ones. Use a better sense of conviction to conquer them.

WHY ANXIETY HAPPENS

Why Anxiety Happens

MANY PEOPLE DESCRIBE "ANXIETY" as a sense of pain. Some describe it as fear involving a state of mind. Fear is part of our panic response, but fear and anxiety are somewhat different. Shock tells us you're in real danger, and you're right to feel you're in danger. Anxiety, on the other hand, is about emotions that are negative. There is a feeling of uncomfortability, even if there is no risk. Anxiety gives you an enhanced fear that something bad will happen, e.g., the chance that someone will come out and scare you. Anxiety responds to things with our instincts and instinctual existence. It happens when we first meet somebody, and something doesn't feel right. Another example is going down a dark alley alone and raising our senses as if we were on our guard. Anxiety is natural and sometimes helpful. It is the natural reaction of the body to pain. However, when you have an anxiety disorder, depression can become harmful. This is when fear affects your mind and body by fighting depression to the extent that it disrupts most aspects of your life and can last more than six months.

What Are Symptoms Of Anxiety?

THROUGH DEFAULT, when you have intense fear, an anxiety disorder is almost all the time, which can make a recovery very hard. Anxiety can turn into agoraphobia (not able to leave home) or anxiety in extreme cases (90 percent of the time symptoms of extreme sadness). You may be discouraged from being social by an anxiety disorder. It can lead you to avoid things like elevator riding and telephone conversation.

Occasional anxiety is supposed to be a part of life. You might feel anxious when faced with a problem at school, before taking a test, or before making an important decision. Yet anxiety disorders are more than just acute stress and panic. Anxiety does not go away for a person with an anxiety disorder and may get worse over time. Symptoms can interfere with day-to-day activities such as job performance, school work, and relationships.

There are many types of anxiety disorders with different symptoms. The most common types of anxiety disorders include:

Generalized anxiety disorder (GAD)

GAD CAUSES CHRONIC, excessive stress about everyday life. This problem could take hours every day, making it difficult to focus and complete daily tasks. A person with GAD may be overwhelmed with anxiety and feel headaches, stress and nausea.

Individuals with a generalized anxiety disorder (GAD) show extreme anxiety or stress, most days for at least six months, about a number of things, such as personal health, jobs, social interactions, or everyday life circumstances. Fear and anxiety can cause serious problems in areas of their lives, such as social interactions, education, and employment.

Symptoms of a generalized anxiety disorder include:

- Feeling nervous, wound-up, or on the verge
- Feeling quickly exhausted
- Having trouble concentrating; mind goes blank
- Getting irritable
- Having body tension

- Difficulty controlling feelings of anxiety
- Sleep problems, such as trouble falling and staying asleep, restlessness, and unsatisfied sleep

Panic disorder

YOU FEEL a sense of impending doom that results in panic attacks randomly for no given reason. This can result in someone fearing another panic attack, which can make the panic disorder worse.

People with panic disorder have frequent sudden panic attacks. Panic attacks are unexpected bursts of intense fear that come quickly and hit their maximum in a matter of minutes. Attacks can happen suddenly or can be caused, such as a suspected target or circumstance.

People may experience the following during a panic attack:

- Heart palpitations, a pounding heartbeat, or an accelerated heart rate
- Sweating
- Trembling or shaking
- Sensations of shortness of breath, smothering or choking
- Feelings of impending doom
- Feelings of being out of control

Social anxiety disorder (formerly referred to as social phobia)

This is a disease that circles around other people's fear, how others feel of you, how they can judge you. You're afraid people will get you. More than shyness, this syndrome causes an intense fear of social interaction, often motivated by an irrational fear of embarrassment (e.g., saying something stupid or not knowing what to say). Someone with social anxiety disorder may not take part in conversations, contribute to class discussions or offer their ideas, and may be isolated. Panic attacks are a common reaction to anticipated or forced social interactions.

People with social anxiety disorder have a general feeling of intense fear or anxiety about social or performance situations. We were worried that the attitudes and behaviors associated with their depression would be adversely judged by others, causing them to feel embarrassed. Such fear also leads people with social anxieties to avoid social interactions. A social anxiety disorder may present itself in a variety of situations, such as in the workplace or in the school environment.

Phobia

A CERTAIN PERSON, location, object, event, or circumstance is disproportionately afraid.

Phobia is an irrational fear or aversion to specific objects or circumstances. Although it may be reasonable to be afraid in some situations, the anxiety that people with phobias may have is out of proportion to the actual danger created by the condition or artifact.

Those with phobias:

- May have an unreasonable and extreme concern about meeting the feared object or circumstance.
- Take active steps to avoid the feared object or scenario.
- Feel acute intense anxiety about experiencing the feared object or situation.
- Combat certain stimuli or circumstances with intense anxiety.

THERE ARE several types of phobic or phobic disorders. As the name suggests, individuals who have a general phobia are extremely terrified of, and feel particularly nervous about, specific types of things or circumstances. Definitions of common phobias include the apprehension of:

- Flying.
- Heights.
- Specific animals, such as spiders, dogs, or snakes.
- Receiving injections.
- Blood.

Obsessive-compulsive disorder (OCD)

THERE ARE persistent destructive obsessive feelings culminating in a person executing their urges or repeating those actions based on their OCD.

Obsessive-compulsive disorder is a kind of mental illness. Those with OCD may have either obsessive thoughts or impulses or compulsive, repetitive behaviors. Some have obsessions and compulsions. OCD is not about patterns like biting your nails and having negative thoughts. The disorder can influence your career, education, and marriage, and stop you from living a normal life. Your emotions and your actions are beyond your influence.

An obsessive thought, for example, is that your family members might get hurt if they don't put their clothes in exactly the same order every morning. A compulsive practice, on the other hand, might be to wash your hands seven times after touching something that might be filthy. You may not want to say or do these things, but you feel powerless to stop.

A lot of people with OCD understand that their feelings and actions don't make sense. They're not doing it because they love it, but because they can't quit. And if they stop, they feel so bad that they're going to start again.

Obsessions and compulsions can include several different things, such as the need for order and cleanness, hoarding, and intrusive thoughts about gender, spirituality, crime, and body parts.

Obsessive feelings may include:

- Fear of germs or getting dirty.
- Worries about getting hurt or others being hurt.
- Need for things to be placed in the exact order.
- A belief that certain numbers or colors are "good" or "bad."
- Constant awareness of blinking, breathing, or other body sensations.
- Unfounded suspicion that a partner is unfaithful.
- Washing hands multiple times in a row.
- Doing tasks in a specific order each time, or a certain "healthy" number of times.
- A regular check on a locked door, a light switch, and other stuff.
- Need to count things, such as steps or bottles.
- Holding products in an exact order, such as cans with labels facing the front Anxiety of hitting doorknobs, using public toilets, or shaking hands.

Anxiety of separation

THIS IS an overwhelming fear of being away from home (agoraphobic systems) and loved ones.

Separation Anxiety Disorder: Separation Anxiety is often considered to be something that only children are concerned with; however, adults can also be diagnosed with separation Anxiety Disorder. People who have separation anxiety disorder fear that they will be part of the people they are attached to. Children also fear that some kind of hurt or something untoward will happen to their relationship figures while they are apart. Such anxiety drives them to avoid being apart from their attachment figures and avoid being alone. Persons with separation anxiety may have hallucinations about being removed from family figures and having physical symptoms if separation happens or is expected.

Agoraphobia

THIS IS the fear of not being able to escape and be stuck in a situation or location, so a person isolates himself from the outside world.

Individuals with agoraphobia are profoundly fearful of two or more of the following situations:

- Use public transport.
- Being in open spaces.
- Being in enclosed spaces.
- Standing in line or being in a crowd.
- Being outside the house alone.

Individuals with agoraphobia frequently fear these conditions, partially because they feel it might be difficult or impossible to escape if they have panic-like responses or other humiliating symptoms. In the most severe form of agoraphobia, an adult can become housebound.

Selective mutism

A SOMEWHAT UNUSUAL anxiety disorder is intentional mutism. Selective mutism occurs when people are unable to speak in specific social situations, despite having normal language skills. Selective mutism usually occurs before the age of 5 and is often associated with intense shyness, fear of social humiliation, compulsiveness, avoidance, clinging behavior, and temper tantrums. Those who are afflicted with selective mutism are also often diagnosed with other anxiety disorders.

Medical anxiety

HYPOCHONDRIA IS ALSO KNOWN as this. Your well-being is an extreme depression. The person automatically assumes that when a little symptom occurs, they are sick.

Post-traumatic stress disorder (PTSD)

IT OCCURS when a person experiences recurrent flash-backs or subsequent panic attacks with a traumatic event.

Each of the listed anxiety disorders has its own features and signs, but during an anxiety attack, they all show the same initial symptoms. We get an over-whelming wave of tension, concern, and terror when someone has an anxiety attack. Anxiety attacks can come from nowhere, or somebody's emotions and their surroundings can carry it on.

Signs of an anxiety attack are as follows:

- Sensation like you're going to pass out.
- Dry mouth.
- Sweating and overheated.
- Restlessness.
- Distress.
- Fear.
- numbness and tingling.
- heart rate increase.

- shortness of breath (as if you can't breathe) and shock sensation.

PANIC ATTACKS ARE MORE intense than attacks of depression, and although they have similar symptoms, they are not the same.
Below is a list of panic attack symptoms:

- An abnormally fast heart rate.
- Hyperventilation.
- Sudden headache.
- Excessive and uncontrollable shaking.
- Nausea.
- Chest pain (as if an elephant is standing on your chest).
- Feeling out of your body (derealization).

PANIC ATTACKS usually occur with no apparent reason, and the person witnessing it is very frightening. Someone might feel like they're going to have a heart attack and die. We have an amazing feeling of imminent doom.

Disorders of depression have a major effect on your brain and body. Nonetheless, the good news is that you can resolve and decrease panic feelings with the right treatment (doctor or qualified consultation), commitment, and attitude. People with severe depression and an excessive number of attacks of panic and anxiety may need to see a medical psychologist in addition to taking prescription drugs recommended by a doctor. Some days, through natural herbs, nutrients, and minerals, we can get away with our short-term effects. We can get better as long as someone can devote themselves to eating healthier, getting enough exercise (both the brain and body), having a good night's rest, and avoiding things such as drugs and alcohol and caffeine.

How Anxiety Affects The Brain

AT SOME POINT in our lives, everyone experiences fear and anxiety. Fear is an immediate response to a specific threat stimulus. Distress, on the other hand, is a less severe but more persistent reaction to causes of distress that may be identified. Of starters, you may be nervous about the prospect of seeing a snake running through the forest, while you may feel anxiety when you slither immediately in front of you.

In some situations, people can generally feel nervous without really understanding why. Normally, the mind regulates our fears and anxieties without allowing them to mess with our daily functioning. If there is a close danger, various areas of the brain can help us make sense of the threat by amplifying and crushing our anxiety and fear.

For some people, however, depression can be debilitating, and it can interfere with everyday life. Anxiety becomes a concern when these brain areas function poorly (or fail to function) and trigger a flood of unwanted or irrational behavior. Long-lasting depression like this can be treated as an anxiety disorder.

Anxiety disorders, such as panic disorder and social anxiety disorder, may require therapy to allow patients to lead a normal, happy life.

Before recently, scientists believed that a marble-sized brain area called the amygdala was a source of fear and anxiety. Several experiments have shown that apes with damage to the amygdala have been remarkably stoic in the presence of terrifying stimuli (like a close snake). Among people with anxiety disorder, scientists thought that excessive fear and depression are triggered by hyperactive amygdala, a complex cause with a clear result.

Today, however, we appreciate that anxiety is the result of constant talk between a number of different brain regions a fear network. Each brain region induces fear on its own. Alternatively, connections between many brain areas are all essential to the way we experience anxiety.

One possible explanation for how this happens is that the brain is separated into two parts: the intellectual brain and the emotional brain. The frontal lobe, where all our sensations and thoughts come together as one unified experience, is the cognitive brain. The amygdala, which is situated deep inside the heart, is part of the emotional brain. According to this hypothesis, we only feel anxiety when stimuli from the emotional brain overwhelm the rational brain and our consciousness. If you can rationalize that, for instance, snakes are common in the forest you're hiking in (using cognitive brain), then the intellectual brain network overtakes and tames the psychological anxiety network.

For example, an area in the frontal lobe called the Dorsal Anterior Cingulate Cortex (dACC) amplifies the nervous signals coming from the amygdala. If nervous patients are shown images of frightened eyes, dACC and amygdala (among other brain regions) ramp up their noise, inducing intense panic. Individuals without fear show little or no response.

On the other side, another portion of the frontal lobe, called the ventromedial prefrontal cortex, tends to dampen the signals coming from the amygdala. Patients with brain damage to this region are more likely to experience anxiety as the amygdala brakes have been lifted.

Using functional magnetic resonance imaging (fMRI), researchers have shown that these brain regions are involved as people experience anxiety. Nevertheless, the specifics of how these areas operate together are not yet decided. Scientists around the world are still hard at work, chipping away at the complexities of depression and anxiety disorders.

Luckily, there is still a strong reason to be hopeful for nervous clients. Many people with depression benefit from drug therapy, such as antidepressants. Other patients will benefit from behavioral therapy. One type of behavioral therapy involves gradually exposing patients to triggers that trigger their anxiety. With time, patients learn to overcome their depression through these frequent encounters, as these experiences do not contribute to actual harm.

Besides medications and behavioral therapy, psychologists and psychiatrists are also working on new ways to treat depression, using recent findings to inform them. Some scientists are trying to use fMRI brain scans to match patients with certain therapies, as anxiety disorders can vary from person to person. Others use methods such as deep brain stimulation to activate anxiety-inducing brain regions back to a healthier state.

Anxiety also gets worse when somebody has low self-esteem and not much confidence. It's when someone doesn't know how or fails to support them-selves by self-care that depression symptoms and an anxiety disorder's growth become too much to bear. But what is actually going on in the brain that makes the signs of depression worse and out of control the person spiral?

Anxiety usually results from an imbalance between the brain's mental and cognitive components. For a brief, the prefrontal cortex and limbic system stimulate the amygdala, which response to unexpected threats and hazards. This is important in circumstances that are dangerous. Nevertheless, the amygdala is responsible for sending messages to other parts of the brain in non-threatening situations to enable the answer to fight or flight.

When a chemical called cortisol is released, the fight or flight reaction happens, transmitting adrenaline throughout the body. Cortisol and dopamine work together, helping someone see longer distances, running faster, talking and thinking more, and becoming smarter. Helping others get out of a dangerous situation is the planning. If no immediate risk or threat happens, the panic attack of a patient is the product of the adren-aline response. This leaves someone with uncontrollable breathing patterns and tingling extremities.

The amygdala, which is responsible for memory function, is another part of the brain which gives false alerts or too much fear. The amygdala takes on every-thing we see and feel. It then transfers these memories to be processed and recorded in other parts of the brain. The issue about depression or hippocampus is that, except for painful events or anything associated with anxiety or pressure, the hippocampus restricts many memories. In other words, memories are stored deep within the hippocampus that revolves around loss, risk, and danger. Then in the future, those thoughts will be activated.

Good memories are pushed aside about safety, consistency, and stability. To make room for the painful ones, they are processed separately. Having said that, if someone does not seek professional help with their depression or low self-esteem issues, they can find themselves in an endless loop of anxiety and stress that can compress and alter the hippocampus shape. This type of damage to the hippocampus can lead to more painful memories, leading to hallucinations, repeated stimuli over what seems to be nothing, and an accumulation of false signals culminating in panic attacks out of the blue. Good memories are pushed aside about safety, consistency, and stability. To make room for the painful ones, they are processed separately. Having said that, if someone does not seek professional help with their depression or low self-esteem issues, they can find themselves in an endless loop of anxiety and stress that can compress and alter the hippocampus shape. This type of damage to the hippocampus can lead to more painful memories, leading to hallucinations, repeated stimuli over what seems to be nothing, and an accumulation of false signals culminating in panic attacks out of the blue.

What's Actually Happening In Your Brain When You Feel Anxious

YOU KNOW THE FEELING: the nervous tension in your heart, the heightened perception you have of everything that's going on around you, the faint apprehension and discomfort that's panic. But, once the body feels the impact, your mind is already at work. The NIMH Guide to Anxiety Disorders also includes a definition of the cognitive processes at work

Many parts of the brain are central players in the development of fear and anxiety. Using brain imaging technologies and neurochemical methods, scientists have discovered the amygdala and hippocampus play a significant role in most anxiety disorders.

The amygdala

IT IS an almond-shaped construct deep in the brain that is thought to be a coordination channel between the parts of the brain that process incoming sensory stimuli and the parts that perceive these signals. The remainder of the brain may be alerted to the presence of a threat and may cause a panic or terror reaction. Emotional memories stored in the central part of the amygdala that plays a role in anxiety disorders that include very distinct fears, such as fears of cats, snakes, and flight.

The hippocampus

IT IS the part of the brain that encodes the memory for dangerous events. Studies have shown that the hippocampus tends to be weaker in some individuals who have been victims of child abuse or who have been involved in military action. Studies should establish what causes this reduction in size, and what role it plays in nightmares, clear memory deficits, and distorted memories of traumatic events related to PTSD.

Feeling anxious is part of your body's stress response. Your fight or flight reaction is activated, and your body is saturated with norepinephrine and cortisol. Both are designed to give you a boost to vision, reflexes and acceleration in dangerous conditions. They raise your heart rate, get more oxygen to your muscles, get more water to your lungs, and basically get you ready to deal with any danger. The body is turning its full attention to life. Ideally, when the risk disappears, it shuts down, and the body goes back to normal.

Benefits Of The Need To Change Your State Of Mind

ONE OF THE first and easiest ways for managing depression is to change your mind. Change your way of seeing yourself and build trust by focusing on your self-esteem and autonomy. Understanding how to calm your mind and focus on what matters to you can have a major impact on how you choose to react to difficult situations. We can find it extremely difficult to relax and alleviate our pressure if we injure our hippocampus and amygdala. As stated, this results in the expectation of stress and anxiety. You should make it a point to understand more about yourself by modifying your attitude and consciously changing how you react to stressful situations in order to counteract these effects.

The advantages of learning how to change your thinking are described below:

Mindfulness becomes easier

YOU MAY MAKE a few errors or become easily distracted when you first begin to meditate and be aware of your surroundings and what is happening in your body. Awareness will help you unwind, relax and improve your way of seeing things through training. You'll have to put all your attention to your breath at the end of your session. Through time, when you develop your mindfulness meditation, by paying attention to your emotions, you can focus on retraining your brain. The more committed you are to retrain your brain, the better it becomes to be aware of it.

Improved immune response

IT SHOULD ONLY TAKE ABOUT eight weeks to adjust the electrical activity in the brain as much as mindfulness needs to be practiced on then developed over time. This means that in just eight weeks, it is possible to reverse the symptoms of a weakened hippocampus and amygdala. Nonetheless, after eight weeks, it is important not to quit because the effects of mindfulness can have a positive impact on your way of life. In 2003, there was a report supporting this hypothesis. The research also explored the effects of meditation, including changing your mind, and it has been shown that meditation can lead to an increased immune response. Those who can sleep and calm their brains are less likely to get sick and get the flu.

A drop in chronic pain

WE ARE what we are talking about, and we are behaving on the grounds of how we choose to react to things. All this is happening in our heads, and we can actually change how our bodies react to physical pain, such as joint and bone pain. Scientists conducted a study on people who tried to change their minds. The results showed that discomfort in the people who focused on mindfulness to regulate their attitude, such as a slight shock to the body, was lower compared to those who did not.

Although not a full list of advantages, you can see how focusing on your brain by carefulness and mindfulness strategies, among other approaches, can really improve your state of mind, contributing to the reversed effects of depression and stress-induced brain damage.

Things To Consider When Using Strategies To Change Your Mind

WHILE YOU ARE WORKING to build self-confidence and self-esteem, you must first consider the realities. Take into account the following list while using strategies to change your mind.

You're not in the past

YOUR PAST EXPERIENCES do not determine who you choose to be or who you are. Anything someone else has said to you doesn't describe you. Let go and breathe from this preconceived notion. Understand that at this point, you are who you want to be.

You are better than what your inner critics try to tell you

THE IRONY of our inner self-hatred, which imposes such high expectations and goals that we are not going to achieve, is that these are all just emotions. Negative emotions like these are not supposed to control the way we perceive the universe because they are all fake. Trust is about being certain that our life is not influenced by the negative thoughts that emerge in our minds. Your feelings may cause you to feel bad, but emotions do not dictate who we want to be either like minds. Combined with your imaginative positive attitude, your pessimistic thoughts and emotions make up who you want to be. That makes you who you are in every part of you. Through these false perceptions, achieving personal growth and overcoming your depression is what helps you to aspire to be who you want to be.

The assumptions of other people about you are wrong

IN MOST SITUATIONS, how somebody views you is their own experience, and that's rarely true. A person n with high self-esteem recognizes that the opinion of some-body about them is just false self-projections. You may have shared your thoughts and told your mates about things that happened to you, but that doesn't mean you're who you are the way we see you. We didn't walk in their shoes or have lived their lives. We can send you advice and encouragement, but only you know how to think, interpret, and feel about your particular circum-stances and experiences.

Self-worth is just how you want to accept it

WHAT THAT MEANS IS that if you think you're worth it, you're worth it. You tell the mind that you deserve less when you settle down for less. The mind will draw on your emotions and thoughts in this situation to help you develop this way of thinking. When you believe you're worth it and choose to focus on taking better care of yourself, your perceptions will change, and so will your self-worth sense.

Sometimes it's all right not to feel all right

MOST OF THE TIME, we get in our heads because we don't give enough credit to ourselves. They also think we're bad if they feel bad. The reality is that we don't have to deny those emotions if we feel bad. We have to sit with them and work kindly and without judgment with them. To admit that your heart is broken or that you feel betrayed or that you are not all right is a human being. So be all right with not being all perfect.

You're an ongoing work

ALL YOU'VE DONE SO FAR HAS made you who you are today, the better and the terrible. It doesn't determine who you want to be and who you want to be. Living is about risk-taking while learning how to concentrate on what matters most. You have to give yourself time to focus on yourself and also be praised when you've made progress. Be careful and kind to yourself as you're a liberal role, and you're not flawless. It's not ideal to be optimistic and self-worthy. On the road, we must accept our faults.

All we've got is now

THAT'S the last thing you need to remember. The history is completed and uncontrollable, while the future is never set in stone for sure. While today on this. Take a single step at a time. This is how you can actually change your way of looking at yourself and cure your depression.

CHALLENGING YOURSELF

Set goals for yourself

IT'S NOT enough to imagine, "I'm going to go out there and not be afraid!" that's not really a concrete target, like thinking, "I want to be amazing." You need action-oriented goals, like talking to a stranger or talking to a cute boy or girl you know. (We're going to cover these actions in the next section).

Focus on little, daily successes, and slowly get more daring. Even telling a stranger, the time could be a daunting task. Don't write off the small chances that they're no big deal! You can work up to talk a little in front of huge crowds. Slow down, man!

Find out what's comfortable with you

STRAIGHT UP, moshing at a party and partying at a club all night long may not be something for you that has nothing to do with shyness. If you'd rather trim your grandma's toenails, listen to that. Don't try to conquer your shyness in the environments you can't stand up. It's not going to stick.

You don't have to do what everyone else does. And if you do, you're not going to stick with it, and you're not going to find anyone that you like and are like you. Why do you waste your time?! If the bar scene isn't for you, that's all right. Practice your social skills in coffeehouses, in small gatherings, or at home. They're more important to your life.

Practice putting yourself in not so comfortable positions

WE DON'T WANT you in positions where you're sitting in the corner, pinching yourself to ease your social discomfort, but you do need to put yourself in situations where you're just a step or two away from your environment. How else are you going to grow?

Start at the top of your list, remember that? It could be talking to a CVS girl, stopping a person at a bus stop for a while, or chatting with the guy who's got the cubic next to yours. Most of the characters are bad at the outset (have you found out why this is yet? They're just like you), but there are openings for conversation.

Introduce yourself to a new person every day

IT IS OFTEN EASIER to talk to strangers, at least briefly. You can never see them again, after all, so who cares what they think of you? This man is walking down the street to the train. Try to make eye contact and smile for him. It's basically three seconds of your life.

The more you do so, the more you find people open and polite. Once in a while, you'll get an odd character who's paranoid who asks why you're laughing at him to think he's all fun to mess with. What's more, smiling makes people wonder why you're smiling now, instead of going the other way around, you're getting in their heads!

Put yourself out there

TALK to someone you don't normally think about having a conversation with. Try to find people who share one or more of your interests and intend to speak to them. You'll find yourself in front of a team at some point or another. Chime in with even the most common comments (or in defense of someone else's). Get acquainted with it. This is the only way to grow.

This is going to get easier over time. Remember how hard it was to drive or ride a bicycle at first? It's the same thing about social interactions; you just haven't had a lot of practice. After a while, you're all going to be "gone, done that." Nothing's going to phase you out.

Count your successes and keep going

WRITE down your achievements in that journal that lists your social causes. Seeing the success you have made is a huge motivation to keep working. In a couple of weeks, you'll be astounded by the power you're handing back, persuading you all the more that this idea is feasible. Great, guy.

There's no timetable for this. It's not going to happen to some people until a lightbulb shines on it, and all of a sudden they get it. For others, it's a long road that lasts six months. However long it takes, it takes as long as it takes. Trust yourself. You're going to get there.

Escape Inner Critic's Anxiety

THE INNER CRITIC is like the manipulative part of you. It's the inner feelings that make you try to believe what it tells you. It asks you things like "You're not good enough," "You're such a loser," "No one loves you," "Why would you be admitted when other candidates are present?" What's so different about you?" Sound familiar with these things? Do you blame yourself for uncontrollable things? In a completely positive case, would you pick out the negatives? This is your criticism inside. It is the part of us that gives life to our insecurities and internal weaknesses. The critic inside seeks perfection and is a teller of fortune. And have you heard that it can also read minds?

The internal critic should never be taken seriously because he is not successful, and he is never honest, even though he seems to tell the truth. When coping with the internal critical part of you, one thing you should always consider is that you are who you believe you are. So if you listen to your inner critic reminding you that you're not good enough, then the idea that you're not good enough will transform into your truth, resulting in fear of chances and obstacles. When you say, "I may think I'm not good enough, but I know I'm good enough, because I know my own strengths and weaknesses," so you agree against your inner critic, which can build trust.

Think about it this way, although your subconscious might sound like it supports you by pointing out your shortcomings, it's really your brain's anxiety component that prevents you from being hurt or upset. It's trying to stop insulting you. When we listen to it, it means only that we give in to our own minds ' fear. How are you going to escape this reality? Say your questions and say yourself if what you'd say to a close relative or a beloved friend is the internal critical voice within your mind. Perhaps not, and if you did, you'd more likely lose your close friend, contributing to loneliness. If that doesn't sound fun to you, here's what you can do to stop your internal critic's terror.

Adapt

IT MAY SOUND CONTRADICTORY, but you can create an image of what that part of you is trying to say about you when we settle in with our inner critic. It may help to draw it out or maybe write it down, but ask yourself questions about the inner critic. How old do you hear your voice? (How old were you when you were first picked?) Who looks like this bully? Sounds like a person from your history (for example, a relative, a spouse, a foe, or an ex-partner)? Will anyone who is in your life now sounds familiar? Painting a photo and knowing more about your inner critic will help you figure out the source and the cause.

Consider yourself interested

HOW OFTEN DOES the inner criticism appear? Where is it quieter than usual in your life? It may sound like it's always there, but it's most definitely not there. If you think you're referring to your inner critic, find out what you're doing right now. In social situations, is it loud? Did you make an error that caused you to become imperfect? Is it telling you to stay home when you're out, or is it forcing you to stop things that you enjoy? Consider how often it happens and be curious about it. In order to see the signs and identify the symptoms, it may be best to keep a diary for when it happens.

Ask more questions. Once you've developed an image of this "ghost" and worked out how often this happens, you can begin to notice stuff you've never seen before about it. Ask things like the following when this happens:

- May I help you?
- What would you like me to know?
- If I don't follow your advice, what are you afraid of that could happen to me?

- What is your reasoning behind these hurtful words?

TREAT your opponents as a tyrant as you would. But be patient, curious, subconscious, and observant.

Listen, then speak

RECOGNIZE the answers after the questions have been answered, and either ask it another question or answer the answer. By convincing it or acting on what you think, you will respond to your inner critic. For example, if the voice said it's afraid that your disappointment will make you even more depressed, respond with "I hear your worry, but I'm not going to allow myself to live in fear of making mistakes" or "I'm not going to go where I need to go in my life." You train your brain to counteract and silence the inner critic when you do this. Should also let the inner critic know it's been noticed, and you're controlling it instead of allowing it to influence should.

As crazy as you may feel speaking to yourself, the less your voices disturb your life, the more you respond to your inner critic. You will slowly notice a difference in your attitude and behavior. Try to have fun with it and let go of your anger while you retrain your opponents to calm down and be less of a nuisance.

Fear Of Failure

THE ONE THING about failure is that we need failure to help us learn from our mistakes and develop into self-confident, self-loving people we are. Performance allows us to be different, and our lives need to move on. If we lose, though, we can feel emotions that arise from our losses, such as disappointment, resentment, sorrow, remorse, guilt, and humiliation. Although these emotions are uncomfortable, a purpose is served by every emotion (whether negative or positive). There are many reasons for our fear of failure. These are the following reasons:

- You may feel judged or fear being rejected if you fail.
- You are afraid of losing people because of your failures.
- You worry excessively over your failure (inner critic) in an attempt not to do it again.
- You beat yourself up over it.
- You worry about disappointing others

THE TRUTH IS that no one is perfect, and the fear of failure can stop you from progressing because you hold yourself too high of expectations. Perfectionism is not about all the time being perfect, but rather minimizing problems so that you are not going to make mistakes. Truly, mistakes are bound to occur regardless of how hard you try to stop them. Acceptance of who you are, regardless of what you do, produces success and ingenuity in managing the fear of failure. Once you're able to accept that you're going to make mistakes because you're human, you will eventually begin to grow and shift your attitude towards disappointment. You can conquer the fear of failure. Here are a few directions.

Possess your fear

YOU MAY FEEL ashamed and regretful when you are scared ashamed of the mistake you made and regretful that, to begin with, you shouldn't have done it. These are false beliefs, however. It is not accurate that it is inappropriate anything less than fine. Accept your worries and understand that you are fulfilling a reason with every emotion you feel. Feeling ashamed will help you remember the incident and stop making the same mistake again. Feeling sorry helps you understand that, when making a mistake, you feel wrong. Understanding right from wrong is a positive feature of establishing relationships, and it can take you through many of your life circumstances.

Think before you do anything or utter anything

THE ONLY WAY TO avoid defeat is to learn about all the options behind your decision and then find a solution. At the time, be careful not to get too trapped because overthinking would get you nowhere. Get to a trustworthy friend or loved one and offer and explain your situation to them in order to gain more perspective. Write down all the reasons behind each direction and formulate the logic. Do not be afraid to fail until you find a solution. Failure is another part of life that makes you develop in your personal growth.

Be contrite

SAY SORRY WHEN you hurt yourself and others. Training to express your failure's outcomes is probably the best way to overcome your anxiety. Understand that you're not great and that you're cool with not everyone getting along or having the same view you're doing. The causes for loss have not been done intentionally, and that is why they are considered failures.

Let go of the hold

MAYBE THIS MOVE is the secret to conquering your fear of failure. One should reflect on the present moment by letting go of what you cannot manage (e.g., the future and events that have already happened). Just what you want to do right now is the only time that counts. Even after planning your course of action to prevent defeat, something unforeseen always comes up that changes everything. You might have made a promise to a friend that you'd come for their birthday, for example. You couldn't stop this if you didn't make it because of a family emergency or because the weather was bad. Rather than seeing it as a loss, make individual plans to fix it with them.

Stay conscious

FEAR OF FAILURE may result from too much anxiety about the future or from preventing what happened in the past at all costs. Such issues are out of your power, as said in the previous step. Rather, all you can do is be fully aware of your actions, emotions, and what you can manage. Also, being observant helps you, so you can be "conscious" of what happened and make mental notes of it. Relax and don't treat it all like a big deal. It's all you can do right now to learn from your mistakes.

It's all right to be afraid

IT HELPS you stay on watch and alert about what's to come. Nobody can predict the future, however, not even your inner critic. Let go of what it is difficult to do, and be one with yourself. Try to create inner peace so it won't be such a disaster if you fail. Understand that you're just normal and that you're doing your best. When you develop your self-esteem and trust, it will seem as if fear of failure is a thing of the past.

AWAKE LOVE AND GRATITUDE FOR YOURSELF

Awake Love And Gratitude For Yourself

SELF-LOVE AND SELF-ESTEEM go hand in hand. Self-love is about taking care of your body, mind, and spirit to the degree that you feel happy and content with yourself. Self-appreciation is the desire to understand everything you've got, what you've worked for, and everything you're as a human. Appreciating who you mean accepting who you are and expanding on your cornerstone that has already been planted. Self-esteem is about learning to feel special, recognizing individuality, and being a person above average. Self-appreciation, though, also helps you to accept everything you are. There is no definition of self-appreciation as accomplishing something or fulfilling your inner desires. It's simply accepting and appreciating why you're the way you're now.

Most people think that building trust, having high self-esteem, and loving yourself is selfish; it is not. Between selfishness and self-centeredness, there is a big difference. Self-centered is where you all have to do with yourself and your desires while ignoring other people's needs and wants because it's all about you.

Being greedy means the key goal is to put yourself first while you are still paying attention to others. If you're the one who needs help, you can't help someone in need. If you already have so much on your mind, you can't keep promises as well. The aim of this book is to convince you that you are capable and deserving first of all to work on yourself and to aspire for personal growth. Appreciation is one of the trust and self-esteem facets. It allows you to understand who and what you are doing. This means you can have faith in your instincts, accept your strengths and weaknesses, and be at ease with your own company.

Honor yourself

EVERYONE IS different in their own way, and all too often, because we cannot embrace who we are, we look to others for what we want. The newspaper does not assist with all marketing methods of losing weight and strategy to spice up your love life with the newsletters and magazines. We actively buy into what we ought to be, what we ought to behave, and why we are not good enough. Yet true self-esteem comes only when you can truly respect yourself. Come to understand the most human part, including your concepts, feelings, possessions, friendships, desires, and self-image. Understanding to respect all the things that make you who you are will help you view life from a different perspective in order to build on the positive base that you already have.

Spend time on your own

YOU CAN GET to know yourself better if you spend some time alone with yourself. You'll understand what makes you scared, why you're resistant to change, and what makes you feel like you're not strong enough to feel worthy. The desire to be polite and kind to yourself is self-compassion. You have to deal with your inner critic in order to be extra-compassionate so that you can listen to your true self (what's below the self-critic). It is possible to follow self-acceptance in these easy ways:

170

Listen to your inner voice

AFTER ALL THE negative parrot chatter, finding and listening to your true voice will help you find the answers to who you really are. You can learn what is most important to you by tapping into your inner voice, finding out what gets you excited, and working out who you really are and what you really want.

Practice good self-discussion

IT TAKES two minutes in the morning, all day long, or before you sleep at night. Positive self-talk can really help you get over your insecurities, even if you don't believe it. Essentially, by reminding yourself that you can do this, you train your brain to fix the damage to the limbic system. Believe in being good, being decent, being valued, being kind, being special, etc.

Picture the baby inside you

WHEN WE WERE CHILDREN, life was so much easier. We studied limits, power and command. Returning to the perspective of how you see the world as a child will make you enjoy the little things, and you'll be more thankful for what you have right now. Self-appreciation means removing the viewpoint of the perfectionist and preferring instead of a more compassionate way.

Listen to the stories you are telling yourself

WE STILL PUT on ourselves tags such as "I'm nervous for sure," "I'm a survivor," "I'm not going to win," "I'm a disappointment," etc. Self-appreciation is the source of what we want to say about ourselves in our story. So when we convince ourselves we're the perpetrator, we start feeling violated, and without even trying, we become the victim. Reflect on your account. Instead of exaggerating the negative and ignoring the positive, tell your story how it is.

Tell gratitude to yourself

INSTEAD OF BLAMING yourself for mistakes or the misfortunes of other people, say thank you for the things you take for granted. Self-appreciation is about being thankful for a balanced body and mind, praising you for your strengths and natural gifts, and thanking you for your shortcomings. Without first knowing your limitations, you cannot grow inner strength. We take these things for granted. The main difference between self-esteem and self-esteem is that self-esteem is a personal self-esteem evaluation. It's simply judging whether you feel like you deserve respect and admiration or not. Self-appreciation is not about measuring yourself on the basis of what you think you deserve; it is more about loving yourself as you are and being thankful for what you have and what you have been given. And how do you really respect yourself?

Don't pause and hesitate

SELF-ESTEEM NEEDS you to do it. Don't wait to be satisfied with a success or a goal. Don't settle for you or try to be noticed by others. Do it all yourself because you can. Look at what you've got and don't dwell on what you don't get or want to learn more from. You should never be materialistic about these issues. Start by being thankful for the proper functioning of all your limbs and then progress into your internal organs. Thank you for having happiness, and for making it because your life is this way.

Use a word of empathy

IF YOUR INNER critic always pipes up with all you do right, change it by replacing the negative with kind words. Change your way of speaking to yourself by reminding yourself what you'd do to someone you loved. If you're forgetful, for example, or you forgot to do something, acknowledge that you've forgotten. Think of all the times when you were not forgetful, rather than being harsh on yourself, or move on from this experience.

Give yourself a treat

HAVE you worked too hard and never liked working so hard? Note that you are good and capable of your hard work and efforts, and reward yourself with a gift so often. This present, like a favorite treat, a new phone, or a video game, can be materialistic. It may also be that you are giving a work break for yourself. Get a massage or spend time in nature, doing the thing that you most love doing. So long as the purpose behind your gift is not to want something but to give a gift out of self-esteem, you will continue to develop self-esteem.

You should be yourself

JUST BE YOU. Don't try to match anybody's standards or be too good in all you do. Don't be afraid of being judged for fear of your irony and silliness. Don't do anything that you wouldn't usually to please someone else. Just be yourself. Once you learn to let go of the small things and be who you are as a person, self-appreciation is established at its strongest point. Be an introvert if you're an introvert. If the party's life is easy, then do that. Don't justify who you are, but just respect who you are.

Those who try so hard never really find out who they are to please others. Then, we slip into the press pit trying to shape who they think other people want them to be. Self-esteem is about discovering what really pushes you to excel and motivates you. What are your hobbies? What are your expectations and goals? What will make you who you are and what will help you feel about yourself at best? It will help you develop self-appreciation by answering these questions through your acts.

Wake Up Your Love For Yourself

WE EXPLAINED IN CHAPTER 2, what self-love was and why building self-esteem and self-confidence is important. Everyone has a different meaning of self-love regardless of the original definition and how I defined it, as it is interpreted differently for each person. Everyone has their own way of showing that they love others, so the concept of "self-love" is based on how someone shows self-love. The problem is, how are you treating yourself?

Set aside the time to love yourself

YOU HAVE to shut off all distractions and pamper yourself to do this properly. Through rubbing lotion on them and massaging them, so they feel better, you can moisturize your feet. Take a long soak of essential oils and salts to really bask in smell, sound, and mind. Make a gourmet meal for yourself. Whatever it feels like to pamper yourself, do it without distractions.

180

Do something you're feeling good about

THIS MIGHT BE something you're good at, or you're just learning how to do something new. A nature walk with your family, a road trip with your cat, a night at home in front of the fire, or just doing something you want to do consciously will help you feel self-love. It can really boost your self-confidence when you do something that you are good at, which in effect increases your self-esteem.

Find the religion inside you

SPIRITUALITY TELLS us things that we have never before known about ourselves, such as our deepest thoughts, greatest impulses, and raw emotions. You're learning how to be the most honest you by embracing your faith and taking a trip that will help you stay focused on what you choose to believe in.

Arrange to compare

WHEN YOU SEE other couples start a family or someone gets married, note that they also have their own issues. Just because it seems like life is good for someone doesn't mean it's perfect. Including you, everybody is suffering. No one has a better lifestyle than anybody else. Yeah, you may not have graduated, or the job you enjoy may not be working. You might wish you had children, but you couldn't have any. Unlike most other people, you may have a disability, and you become envious of their lives. Keep in mind that just because someone has a white picket fence, three children, a happy marriage, and a well-trained dog doesn't mean they didn't work to get there. Remember self-esteem? This is the moment to be grateful for what you've got. Know that you are capable and confident enough in life to get anything you want.

Choose your altar

YOUR REFUGE COULD BE AS imaginative as physically going to a place in your head where you find comfort and safety, or a place in the universe that is real. Think of a time you feel the best and happiest. Picture this place in your head and actually go there. Let go of the other problems in your life when you're there. Without the extra stress and job pressure, just concentrate on this happy place. This is how, at its best, you can exercise self-love.

Chase the visions you have

A DREAM IS a vision that somebody is trying to fulfill by the end of their lives. The fantasy of somebody might be that on a large farm, they surround themselves with livestock and live off the land. The vision of another person might be to become famous and popular for something in the world. Dreams are not achieved most of the time because we do nothing to take a step towards it. Sit down and find out what your dream is, and then work back to how you can get it. You should see the instructions on how to follow your goals when you're done.

Self-love is about knowing that love is necessary and that no one can give it to you. You may need to exercise these self-loving methods when you feel that you slip into relationships too easily or that you rush into work when you're overwhelmed or don't allow yourself enough time to think about what's most important to you. Nobody knows how to love you more than you do, and you know how to love the best of yourself. When you struggle to find reasons to support yourself, go back and figure out how to show love to others. The reason we treat someone else is the way we want to be loved most of the time.

Turn Yourself From Who You Are To Who You Want To Be

WHETHER IT'S WORKING out what you're most excited about, creating a stronger sense of trust, discovering your true identity, and following long-term goals that you may not be who you want to be today. As true self-esteem means you fully accept yourself for who you are and what you perceive yourself. It's also every day about creating and rising. Here are places you can really liberate yourself from what holds you back and try to become who you always wanted to be.

See yourself in a different light. You are an artwork, and the sooner you understand it, the easier it will be for you. First, you have to recognize who you are as a person, then find out the things you most want to focus on without judgment. It is as if it were an artist. We take a step back while we draw to work out what they can improve and what they need to concentrate on. Look in this direction at yourself and change something without emotional attachment.

Consider the corresponding pattern of the item you'd like to alter

YOU CAN STRUGGLE to change what you want to change if it's related to or connected to a specific addiction. First, you have to figure out what this habit is, and start by modifying the habit. It's like those gumdrops; before you can get to the gooey good part, you have to eat the candy around the gum.

Set goals that are rational and attainable

CHOOSE something you want to alter, such as a smoking habit or a question of self-esteem. Start from the bottom and work your way to change it completely. If it's a question with self-esteem, you're in the right place now. Just find out where to start and what you're going to commit to every day in order to achieve your small goals.

Surround yourself with real and genuine people

THOSE WHO WANT the best for you and understand that you're focusing on yourself alone to turn into who you want to be, don't just say yes all the time. Authentic people really value you and challenge you constructively. We listen and watch your success to encourage you and help you find out more about your personal growth.

If you really want to change who you are, you need to commit yourself to this transition every day. You have to invest in hard work and not give up when things get tough. Be prepared to take chances and embrace the uncertain future. It is better to handle the transition and be willing to adapt to it so that you can be more confident in further striving. The quality you want to become is that it won't happen overnight. In reality, when the change happened, you may not even understand or remember. Eventually, one day at a time will take you to a day in the future that you will be able to look back and remember everything you have done so far.

ESTABLISHING A
STRATEGY

Establishing A Strategy

BUILDING trust and self-esteem are part of changing your life. You also have to change your behavior if you change your life. It can be very hard to stick to when we start a new schedule. You need to learn how to develop new patterns that transform into a routine to start a new practice. It's better for most people to start with a morning routine and then gradually increase their routine into a full day, including nighttime. But the challenge with creating a plan and learning to work with it is sticking to it in order to bring about a change in your life. We are so used to doing what we've always done that if we're not vigilant, our old habits will begin to take over our new ones. There are a few things to keep in mind when modifying your routines and behaviors during the process:

- Build yourself a regular bonus to stick to your new routine.
- Pay yourself for the success you have made after each month.

- Start small, and at the same time, one new thing.
- Use a physical reminder to continue doing your new daily routine, like when you wake up in the morning and leave your running shoes on the toilet at night.

HERE ARE a few more things you can do to stick to your new daily schedule before diving into building one for reasons of self-esteem and trust:

Link the new routine to your current one

IF YOU CAN LINK it to something else, it is much easier to stick to something. This is because our minds are conditioned and educated in a manner that will set you up for more mistakes to do something completely new. Include a morning sprint to your already usual morning run if you want to consider getting more exercise in your day. If you like journaling, add a calendar to your journaling habit and build a plan for the next day.

Develop self-consciousness

THIS HELPS you to sort out why your previous habits have not worked out when you develop self-awareness by being conscious of the present moment. In every moment, mindfulness is about being present so you can be fully aware of it. Being more aware will allow you to understand what works and what doesn't. The perfect routine you like is one you've built to suit your particular needs. You need to ask yourself a few questions to increase your self-awareness, which will provide more insight into why you are modifying your daily routine.

- What will you benefit from this new habit of life?
- What implications will this new routine have in your life and positive side effects?
- What is the outcome that will allow you to do or become?
- Which parts of your life will help support this new routine?
- How inspired are you to establish this routine and stick to it?

IN YOUR LIFE, everything you intend to improve has to count and mean something. It must be one thing at a time, and in the long run, you should be able to see your sacrifices paid off. In order not to break, the new habits need to be carefully thought out. The concern with most people is that they read books on self-help and immerse themselves in the methods they have learned without putting a lot of effort into the individual workouts. If you do this with a new habit or routine, you may find that you don't adhere to it down the road a little bit. This may also be because what you are seeking to do is clash with your life and routines that have already been prioritized. When you begin to notice that you are moving back to your old ways, you may want to start looking at why. That's where self-awareness comes into play so you can know it as it happens, not when it's too late, and you have to start again.

Don't think too much about late afternoon. For now, all you're focused on is what you're going to do in the morning to set up your day with the right trust and order. The explanation you have to start with morning routines is that we seem to have so much more strength and motivation to get up and go when we wake up in the morning. The energy we have in our minds is starting to diminish as the day goes by. And make sure you start as near as you can when you wake up and you begin your daily routine.

Don't do it on your own

GET your nearest friends on it too when you do something different. That way, not only will you feel obligated to do it for your mates when you wake up and don't feel like it one day, but they will also inspire you to keep going. So perhaps your mates don't want to lead the same lifestyle as you do, but perhaps they want more exercise. Have a friend at the pool. Have a friend for a healthy diet buddy, another friend for a positive newspaper affirmation buddy, etc. You gain more support when you include your family, which will allow you to excel in the long run.

So, if you make a daily ritual of confidence-building, make a checklist so that at the end of the day, you can carry it out. You can learn everything you forgot right there and then and set it up to do it tomorrow. Creating self-esteem and trust would cause the rest to fall into place as they should — self-respect, self-esteem, self-esteem, appreciation, compassion, etc.

Creating A Confidence-Boosting Schedule

THE THING about successful or confident people that you see or visit with is that they were not born that way. They worked hard at growing themselves and becoming who they want to be. You can do the same thing, too, with practice, dedication, and following the steps on how to keep a new daily routine. The one thing about confident people is that they know that when they procrastinate what needs to be done to work on themselves, they won't get anywhere, or they will just drag themselves back even more.

Before you can start setting a schedule that works best for you, it's best to keep these things in mind to develop self-confidence and self-esteem.

Before anything else, get rid of the inner critic

THE SECTION "FEAR of the Inner Critic" in chapter 6 explains how to get rid of the inner critic and how to talk back to your ANTs (automatic negative thoughts), and these ANTs are the most harmful thing that can slow your personal growth process down. If you struggle with an inner critic, then as soon as you get up, read over your critic journal (negative thought journal) and start rehearsing positive self-talk before you even leave the house. If you haven't already, then start planting sticky notes with positive quotes written on them around your house, especially in areas you can see them. More examples later in this chapter.

Learn new things about your downtime

LEARN new things on your way to work, school, seeing boys, court, etc. Research has shown that if you learn something new outside the office, such as a new language, new spiritual direction, or math formulas, your cognitive happiness improves the same way that an upliftment does. Listen to a language guide on the way to work and play brain games for a bit of fun and inspiration to carry on your day if you really want to see a change in your confidence.

Think. Remember. Apart from the busy morning schedule you're preparing and making, set 10 to 15 minutes aside for yourself. It gets your body up to go and be refreshed. Make sure you're all alone like getting dressed or using the washroom, most likely before your bath or during a routine you're doing alone. Several activities may include being conscious, reminding your-self ten different things that you love about yourself (fresh from yesterday), and writing in your journal of appreciation. When your mind is clear and all the nega-tivity you get out of it, you will begin the day with a clear head and potentially become more productive as you have allowed yourself time to reflect.

Consider yourself

APART FROM THE busy morning schedule you're preparing and making, set 10 to 15 minutes aside for yourself. It gets your body up to go and be refreshed. Make sure you're all alone like getting dressed or using the washroom, most likely before your bath or during a routine you're doing alone. Several activities may include being conscious, reminding yourself ten different things that you love about yourself (fresh from yesterday), and writing in your journal of appreciation. When your mind is clear and all the negativity you get out of it, you will begin the day with a clear head and potentially become more productive as you have allowed yourself time to reflect.

Get dressed

SOMETIMES, if not all the time, dress better than you usually do. Ditch the sweatpants and pajamas and throw on some nice jeans and a shirt with a pin. You will grow a more positive type of attitude when you look good and feel like a professional. It can be a great builder of confidence when others note the change in your look and mood.

Exercise

EXERCISE HAS MANY ADVANTAGES, like how you see yourself gradually, and increases self-esteem. It takes the body about twenty minutes to get into the workout activity and about ten minutes to begin feeling the effects after that. So if you start to do a morning ritual of exercise for up to thirty minutes, you can feel the positive effects on your body and mind. Exercise is one of the main things you can do to reduce the body's stress and tension.

Don't care about what we feel about other men. People are so concerned about themselves and their own life to be too bothered about what is happening in your head. Stop telling fortune and dwelling on what others feel about you or talk to you. Chances are they don't think a lot about you and your troubles and pay a lot of attention to how they feel about you. As sad and surprising as this may seem, the fact is, if you don't care what others think and only rely on your own self-awareness, your trust levels would skyrocket.

Having a complete morning routine for confidence-building should set the ball in motion to make you feel better about yourself. All you have to do with this knowledge is find out what kind of routine you can build on your own. You will feel more confident by the end of the month as long as you get enough rest, hit the snooze button, workout, have some time alone for yourself, and have a well-balanced breakfast. Creating a schedule takes 21 days and then 21 more days to stick to one, so you can grow and adhere to a more regular everyday habit.

This is a schedule for an example:

- Get a good sleep night.
- Wake up, work out, and relax (yoga).
- Have a sumptuous meal.
- Shower, teeth washed, body grooming, etc.
- Think about it or be with you.
- Read a book, magazine, paint, and learn something new.
- Set up what you need to do for your day.
- Implement positive affirmations of self-discussion / daily.

YOU WILL START FIGURING out your overnight routine, which is the opposite of your morning routine, by improving your morning routine about anything that fits for you. When you begin your morning routine with positive self-talk, you do your positive self-talk right after you write for what needs to be done tomorrow during your night-time routine.

How To Build A Routine Of Self Love

SELF-CONFIDENCE AND SELF-ESTEEM ARE SIGNIFICANT, but most people forget to do self-love. You can focus on your confidence, build your self-esteem, introduce self-respect, and develop self-worth, but if you don't learn to love yourself, at the end of the day, all this won't really matter. Self-love is like the glue that holds the self-improvement positivity together. So now that you've built a self-sustaining morning ritual of trust into your day, it's time to learn the next move that brings a bit of self-love into your day. Here's how to:

Apply with purposeful respect
everything you use

ALWAYS TAKE the time to soak it up as you lather lotion on your hair. Massage the essential oil and emphasis on straightening and gelling your hair with care. Talk of good feelings like "I'm important," "I'm exceptional," "I look amazing," "I feel great," etc. when you do this.

Tell yourself one thing you love both morning and night

THIS MAY BE you've done really well in your interview or you've been very supportive to your mate. You may say you love being so empathetic or being thankful for your resilience. If you're not feeling so great today, remember what you've genetically inherited from your family and be glad you've got the trait or attribute from them.

Creating the right plan when you get back

EVERYONE HAS TO WIND DOWN, so switching the Television on or beginning dinner right away is only natural. Nonetheless, try to make yourself the first cup of tea instead of turning the TV on or before you have dinner right away. You might be able to turn into something cozy and relaxing to cuddle up with your dog to have a "me time." Think for a moment because after a long hard day at work you deserve this for yourself.

With thanks, end the day

SO TODAY you've had a rough day traffic jams, burnt food, workplace failures, etc. Make sure that you always start the day with the good aspects of your life. This may be that your wife is caring and helpful, your children are happy, or you have a lot of good friends. Whatever you like, make sure you write it down and ask somebody about it. Who knows, you could also change your day.

As you begin to act on these to-dos, you will see that you begin to feel good for yourself slowly. You feel positive and in control when you feel better. One of a positive person's qualities is that they have no lack of control over their lives. We know what we can't control, and they've learned to let it go. What they can influence is how they enjoy each day more. Wait no longer to feel better and wait for people to pick you up and help you. Self-love is about doing for yourself what you want someone else to do for you. So if you're nervous about love, then lather the lotion. Tell yourself who you love most about yourself if you like compliments. Talk with yourself and send your brain the feelings you've been waiting for if you need help. Self-love will come with time.

HOW TO MAKE GOOD FLASHCARDS FOR DAILY USE

How To Make Good Flashcards For Daily Use

IT'S time to make these flashcards creatively. When you have a bad day or a tough time, flashcards come in handy. It's because when something doesn't seem to work or you just don't want to do today's schedule. Having a day off is fine, but look at the flashcards you made on those days. Paint them in any color and brighten it with sparkles and gel pens. You can put some suggestions on your flashcards here.

- I can also brighten the day of someone else by encouraging myself to be happy.
- I have a great sense of humor to get me to navigate these dark days.
- My wife and I have a bond that I'm not going to exploit.
- I am a person that is positive and well-deserved.
- Lam resilient enough to cope with anything life throws at me.

- I know that because I'm powerful, I can achieve my goals.
- I see anxiety as a threat, not a hindrance.
- It's the start of new successes to come my way today.
- I'm a solver of the problem.
- Lam confident and trustworthy.
- In others, I always see the better because I'm secure enough to know who's helping me in my life.
- My resilience is worth nothing simple. I'm going to tackle the hard times because it's worth the reward.
- Lam is allowing myself to be proud.
- Lam deserving of my life's great stuff.
- I am sure that my instincts and myself will lead me to great things.
- My fight isn't over.
- Life's going on right now.
- Breathe calmly. Exhale drama and uncertainty.
- I'm going to pick peace over war.

THESE ARE JUST a handful of positive statements. You will improve your outlook and attitude when you read these every day, and you can become the strong and confident person you've tried so hard to be.

Here are some thank you quotes to put on your flashcards.

- "Try to be happy for what you already have while finding everything you want" (Jim Rohn).

- "Be glad for what you've got; you're going to get more. When you dwell on what you don't have, you're not going to have enough " (Oprah Winfrey).
- "Only one day, you can look back and realize that they were big things" (Robert Brault).
- "Many people complain about the thorns of roses; I am glad that thorns have roses" (Alphonse Karr).
- "An admiration and motivation is the way to develop the best in an individual" (Charles Schwab).

TO MAKE YOU FEEL BETTER, you may choose to check for quotations and make your own. The goal is to feel strong and confident. You can live vicariously by quotations from others and in what makes you who you are, be one with the world. Trust and self-esteem include learning how to practice self-love and gain self-respect. On those dark days, you accept that it's "one of those days" while also realizing that there are better days to come. The first step has to be taken by you, and it is up to you when you would like to start.

SELF MAINTENANCE

Self Maintenance

TAKING care of yourself may be the most critical part of learning to be more comfortable and have a high degree of self-esteem. Most people think it's just about fulfilling their basic needs to take care of themselves. That's not enough. Self-care is what we are consciously doing to ensure that our minds (mental state), bodies (physical state), and spirits (emotional state and soul-driven state) are stable.

If you have a high level of anxiety, your friendships are on the rocks, your head is strained, or you are overly stressed, that means you haven't cared for yourself well. A good self-care routine means that you have taken enough time for yourself, you eat well-balanced meals, you exercise, you practice mindfulness to develop your mental awareness, and you have a load of supportive people in your life. You feed your body and brain with the foods that you need to be safe and happy if you eat well. You release the extra pressure that is built up in your mind and body as you work-out. You teach yourself to calm and learn to let go of the little things that weigh you down when you meditate. You can release energy and pressure as you write that you don't need. Finally, intimacy, caring, and encouragement are required by every person. You may also feel a sense of inner peace and happiness that restores your heart and religious energies when you surround yourself with positive and supportive people.

Most people have different interpretations of what self-care is and how it should be applied in their lives, but a guide will usually help you understand better.

- Say no to stress, which includes the following:

1. Check emails at night
2. Attending group events just because you feel obliged to them
3. Answering your mobile if you know it's going to be a debate

- Learn to be assertive, which includes:

1. Say no to too many obligations
2. Make too many decisions to bring to your plate
3. Strong boundaries
4. Stand up on your own

- Eat healthy, which includes the following:

1. Adding all the essential vitamins and minerals to your diet
2. Make sure your body is safe

3. Eating balanced meals or small meals through the day

- Get enough rest, which includes:

1. Having seven or eight hours of sleep each night
2. Not having more than three hours of sleep during the day

- Exercise, which includes the following:

1. Learning yoga
2. Doing safe exercises without working out
3. Don't overdo it

- Make sure you are physically healthy, which includes:

1. Check-in with the doctor for advice (if necessary)
2. Check-in with the dentist
3. Take advice appointments (if required)

- Spend time with people you love and care for, which includes:

1. Have no distractions
2. How to give and take
3. Creating a "time for myself."

- Meditate, which includes the following:

1. Finding time for you alone
2. Respond to your thoughts and discuss them
3. Be patient

YOU'VE LEARNED to build an organized routine and daily practice that you do every day. Make sure you add the workouts throughout this section to get the best benefits out of life when you get used to your morning routine. Through having a plan that allows you to take good care of yourself while building self-confidence, you can find that you are generally happier. This is because you give yourself more time to think, more time to focus, and more time for yourself in particular.

LEARN MINDFULLNESS

Learn Mindfulness

MINDFULNESS, also known as meditation, has many advantages that include helping you relax your mind, taking your attention to yourself and your surroundings, and allowing you to alleviate and manage stress in particular. Meditation is where you practice without judgment to be one with your emotions so you can better understand them and undo them and encourage them. Meditation is not the same as being conscious, but it is very much the same. Mindfulness is the art of being at the given moment, fully conscious and aware. At first, it can be hard to get into it if you start practicing mindfulness and consciousness. Although it's simple, meditation takes work, concentration, and commitment as the more you do it, the better it gets. Being non-judgmental is the trick. Do not beat up if, at first, it doesn't work. As you continue to practice mindfulness, it will become smoother, leaving you with incredible results, which in the long run, will make you feel better mentally and emotionally. Meditation of meditation should be used on a daily basis. It's like algebra. You'll fail when you stop practicing, and then it's going to be hard to get back on track. You won't see all at once, too.

Generally, meditation is very helpful, and meditation on consciousness is the most effective. As we cultivate mindfulness, we develop the ability to return to the present moment and to retain it. Moving into mindfulness takes three easy steps:

Stay relaxed

SIT in a chair and lie down comfortably. Make sure your belly is flat and open for breathing. Remember the body and do what makes you feel the most relaxed. Your eyes are closed. Hold them focused on a focal point and concentrate on your intake.

Concentrate on your breathing

TRY NOT TO MANIPULATE IT. Only focus on where it comes from. Does it come from your nose and your stomach? Attempt not to change the pace. Mind your breath. Imagine the air sound.

Achieve this for two or more minutes

IF YOUR EMOTIONS distract you and you feel bored by the quiet silence, be mindful that this has happened and turn your attention back to your breath. If it works, you can use an Internet and stress software breathing ball workout to concentrate on your breath. You'd take a breath as the ball spreads. You'd breathe out as it contracts.

You can now be curious about it once you complete your first session of this quick and simple exercise. How long have you been busy before? During this process, was your mind busy? Have you ever tried to think about something in particular? That's natural. This is essentially what should happen because we are first telling ourselves to reflect on the moment while being careful with our brains. They are confused about what deserves the most attention as our thoughts drift. When we learn better to return our attention to our breath, then we can learn how to control our emotions and react appropriately to them. We always have to conclude the workout with our breaths being refreshed and finished on a positive note. When you feel stressed, that's when you'd take your focus back to the air and wait patiently to calm down. Such sessions can take up to 5 to 30 minutes or more anywhere.

The Advantages Of Exercise

PHYSICAL EXERCISE ALLOWS you to keep your mind stable and calm. It allows you to become safer mentally. However, tests have shown that it also allows you to live longer. Exercise can battle hypertension, cardiovascular disease, and complications with the heart and lungs. In the long term, it is also good for nutrition. Physical benefits of exercise include:

- Weight management.
- Decreased risk of heart attack.
- Lower blood cholesterol levels.
- Decreased blood pressure.
- Production of stronger bones, muscles, and joints.
- Reduction of muscle stresses.
- Improved morale, strength, and relaxation.

THE EFFECTS that exercise has on your mental health are as follows:

- Helps with anxiety.
- Blocks negative thoughts that distract you from daily activities.
- Increase social reinforcement when you workout with a friend.
- Enhances sleep and the amount of rest you receive.
- Increases good chemicals and reduces toxic chemicals in your brain, such as serotonin, endorphins and stress hormones.

TARGETING at least 30 minutes of exercise a day is great. You may find that you feel hungry as you do exercise a routine. Use things that improve you instead of giving you high sugar before you fall. Foods such as green tea, bacon, meat and green vegetables are these.

It doesn't matter what kind of workout you're doing. Note not once to do the same workout. For starters, one day, the next day, when you exercise your muscles, aim to reinforce them. Have a body team every day that you're working on. For example, you're working on your arms one day. Then, if you choose to work on your legs or stomach, give them a break the next day. Practicing yoga is the most effective workout.

Develop Better Skills For Socialization

RESEARCH HAS SHOWN that positive socialization encourages people who are stronger and healthier. It makes sense because they have a support system behind them when they look at people who are genuinely happy. The old saying goes something like, "Raising a baby takes a village." In all ways, this is real. Whether you're just looking for help in managing social anxiety or phobia, or just looking for a night for a guy or a night for a girl. Friends and family, when we're sad, happy, upset, irritated, etc. We're looking for those to share our joy with when we're in a good mood. We're waiting for our loved ones to wind up when we're sad or upset. Certain socialization advantages include:

- This relieves symptoms of depression and anxiety.
- Because of the joy they experience, it creates a strong immune system.
- You can concentrate better and focus better.
- This fosters self-esteem and confidence.
- It reduces pressure.

OF EXAMPLE, this is not a complete list, but if you notice that in your life you are surrounded by negative people, it's time to look at what kind of friends you want to be around you. If you have toxic mates who drain all your energy and feel the reverse of these advantages, then the people around you need to be re-evaluated. During group settings or social events, do you sometimes feel socially awkward? Maybe that's because you can lack effective communication skills. If this sounds like the case, here are some qualities to focus on:

Pay attention

WHEN YOU'VE TALKED TO, switching off all distractions. Make sure the phone is off, the radio doesn't play in the background, and your attention is focused on the person you're talking to. Most people hear what they are being told without actually listening. This leaves them incapable of understanding what is being said. A big reason why this is is that we are in the age of technology and our main focus is on telephones or other devices. Be very mindful of how you use the apps while traveling to get a better perspective and have closer relationships.

Comprehend

TO BE empathic towards the opposing party, you don't have to understand something fully; but, you need to try to understand what's being said. You can gain a better understanding by listening with your full attention and rehearsing what they said back to you. We will be more open and willing to hear you speak as well when we feel that you understand them. Others like to lead by example, and you show self-respect in what you want to do to you as well, because you set a good example.

Be empathetic

AS WE PLUNGE into conversations with people, they sometimes react too fast, disrupt the other person, and don't get the relationship idea entirely. If the other party is compassionate and empathic, they will encourage you to talk, but they will leave the conversation dissatisfied. Follow them as empathetically as possible throughout the communication.

Here are some tips for an empathic communicator:

- Refrain from directing the conversation toward yourself.
- Do not try to interpret the other person's experiences.
- It's not a competition. Do not one-up the individual with your own experiences that seem better or worse than theirs.
- Do not dismiss the other's feelings as less than or say, "Don't be sad because ..." and change the topic.
- Give them empathy; do not give sympathy.

Be responsible

IF THE OTHER person has hurt your feelings in any way, bring this up to them, but do not blame them for making you feel upset. Be responsible for your own actions and take credit for your own thoughts and feelings. They may have triggered the emotions, but they are not the cause of them. For example, rather than saying, "You are so unreliable, and for that, you have made me so angry," you could say, "I am upset with you because I was under the impression our agreements are promises we stick to. Can you please make sure this doesn't happen again?" The tone of the conversation will change if you are responsible rather than victimized.

Be careful with your body language

COMMUNICATION IS NOT ALL about words. Body language, such as facial expressions, tone of voice, and posture, or gestures, are part of it too. When you are talking, make sure your body language matches what you are saying; otherwise, you could come off as confusing. Being confused or reading into mixed messages are never fun, and it might seem as though you are playing games, which can hurt your relationship.

Effective communication is key when building long-lasting love relationships. When you are heard, they understand. When they are heard, things go much smoother. When you ask for something from someone, make sure to use clear and concise language rather than beating around the bush. Someone is more likely to give you what you need when you are upfront and direct about it.

You have now learned how to conquer your doubts, follow a new routine, rid yourself of the dark inner critic, and build ways to become more comfortable. It's your decision what you're doing with the information provided in this book, but go ahead and tag your favorite chapters and read more to develop self-esteem and confidence. Just note that this is your career, and you're going to choose what you're going to do with it. No matter what you choose to do, what you agree on your path from here, note that self-confidence is not about suppressing your negative thoughts, but about realizing what you deserve. Self-esteem is about focusing on what you want, and going after what you want, but having the confidence to do it. This workbook of self-confidence teaches you self-love, motivational affirmations, and meditation techniques, because being who you are is vital. Stop wasting time on people who don't support you and start supporting yourself through self-care and inspiration. Your own view is what matters.

The rest of your life is starting right now, and it's entirely up to you to do what you're going to do with all the knowledge you've learned in your life to this level.

Have confidence in everything you do!

Thank you so much for reading my book!

I really appreciated that you chose my book among the many great books about self-help.

I have a small favor to ask: would you leave a review for this book?

Your feedback will help me to make improvements to this book, and to create even better ones in the future.

I love to hear from my readers!

Thanks in advance for your valuable help!

Harry

If you'd like to post a review about this book on Amazon or Goodreads

Printed in Great Britain
by Amazon

34766746R00210